10-28-1466 Rotterdam
Holland
7-12-1536 Basil, Switzerland
of
dysentery   Catholic Priest

THE

ENCHIRIDION

OF ERASMUS
of Rotterdam
Translated bible in to
Greek

D1431557

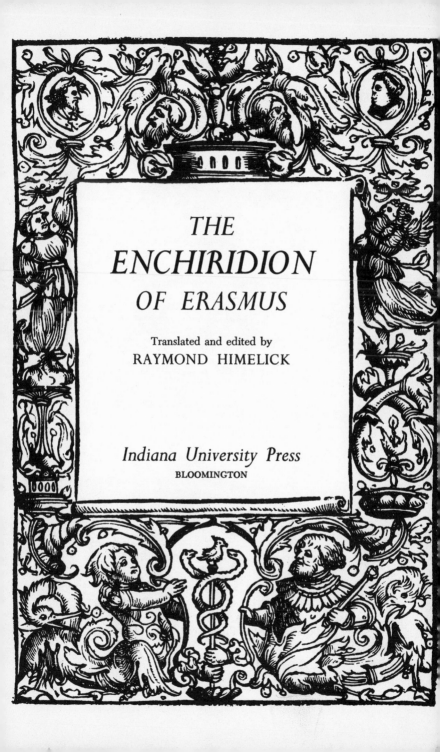

THE
ENCHIRIDION
OF ERASMUS

Translated and edited by
RAYMOND HIMELICK

Indiana University Press
BLOOMINGTON

Note

The translator has used a first edition of the *Enchiridion militis Christiani*, by Johann Froben, printed at Basle in 1519. This volume reprinted the *Enchiridion* from the 1503 Antwerp, Lubricat, edition of Erasmus. The translator has supplied descriptive chapter headings.

to
A. C. Judson

ALL RIGHTS RESERVED
Copyright © 1963 by Indiana University Press
Library of Congress catalog card number 63-16615
Manufactured in the United States of America

Preface

NGLISH VERSIONS OF the *Enchiridion militis Christiani* are almost impossible to come by, I have found. But Latin editions of this work of Erasmus of Rotterdam are plentiful. This is a situation which I am now making an attempt to remedy, by supplying what I hope is a readable and accurate translation of a very significant Renaissance document, with enough editorial assistance to be useful, say, to the interested non-specialist.

Even so modest an undertaking, of course, puts one in debt. Summer grants from the Purdue Research Foundation, for instance, were of material help in preventing a slow business from becoming even slower. My colleagues, Professors C. E. Eisinger, Harold Watts, and Robert Lowe, have shared with me their critical judgment and experience in appraising the manuscript. I am especially indebted to Professor Rudolph Gottfried for his meticulous checking of a very substantial portion of my translation against the Latin text— and his conclusive demonstration that even the best-intentioned translator needs someone to pick up after him. Whatever sins remain here must be taken as evidence that my capacity for error has foiled the combined efforts of those who knew better.

Finally, for certain annotations of the text I am indebted to

Ford Lewis Battles' partial translation in *Advocates of Reform* and to the Hajo Holborn edition of the Latin text in *Desiderius Erasmus Roterodamus, Ausgewählte Werke*, Munich, 1933.

RAYMOND HIMELICK

Contents

Introduction

NCHIRIDION MILITIS CHRISTIANI: within its pages are the burning questions of the age of Erasmus, but for us they are only mild historical curiosities. Though our own century is sometimes credited—more hopefully, perhaps, than accurately—with a reawakening of the religious spirit, the reader who addresses himself to the *Enchiridion* today will probably bring to it a kind of built-in difficulty: not in understanding what Erasmus meant, but in the inability to share in the real excitement it seems to have generated among its contemporary readers. True, we have been frequently reminded in recent years that sermons were as much a part of ordinary Elizabethan life as bear-baiting; but one suspects that, privately at least, most of us regard the first enthusiasm as no less remarkable than the second. It would be a rare student who reacted to an exegesis of the complete gospel of Matthew as did young Thomas Platter of the early sixteenth century, who reported that he felt as if he were being pulled up by the hair of his head.[1]

In the Renaissance, however, this heartfelt preoccupation with questions of faith and doctrine did exist, and it helped make the *Enchiridion* a best seller. First published in 1503, it had more than thirty editions within the next twenty years —in French, Dutch, Spanish, German, and English, as well as in the original Latin—and dozens more by the end of the century.[2] Even the Aztecs, it seems, could improve themselves by its instruction in their own language. Although history does not record how eagerly they took to it, the accounts of an English bookseller for 1520 do show that a third of all the sales to his countrymen were of works by Erasmus and that the *Enchiridion* was one of the favorites.[3]

When he wrote the treatise in 1501, however, most of the enormous and varied work which was to earn for Erasmus the handy graduate-school tag "greatest humanist of the Renaissance" was still to be done. He was approximately thirty-five, having been born—although the exact time and place remain uncertain—about 1466, in or near Rotterdam, one of the illegitimate children of a priest. By the turn of the century the bulk of his writing, aside from his *Antibarbari* and some Latin poems, consisted of works on education: *De Ratione Studii, De Copia, De Conscribendis Epistolis,* and some early colloquies which he intended as pedagogical exercises.

Unquestionably the attitudes and thought of the *Enchiridion* were being shaped, at least in part, by his training and experience during the last quarter of the century. As a teenage boy he attended St. Lebwin's school at Deventer, where some of his teachers were Brethren of the Common Life, a lay order emphasizing poverty, simplicity, humility, and devotion rather than dogma or the subtleties of formal theology. To these ideals of simple piety and the ethical orientation of religion it is obvious that Erasmus responded warmly. In his twenties he reluctantly entered an Augustinian monastery at Steyn and after six years was ordained a priest. His distaste for the experience he never bothered to conceal. "Monasticism," as he put it near the end of the *Enchiridion,* "is not piety but a way of living, either useful or useless according to one's moral and physical disposition."[4] He was very sure the

requisite disposition was not his. When he was about thirty
he entered the University of Paris, where he studied theology
and, incidentally, confirmed his dislike for the arid "quiddi-
ties" of traditional scholasticism.

Two years before the writing of the *Enchiridion* Erasmus
went to England, where he met More and Colet, as well as
other eminent figures associated with religious and intellectual reforms. His best known work today, the *Praise of
Folly*, was a tangible result of his friendship with More; the
earlier *Enchiridion* reveals the influence of Colet's advocacy
of faith and self-sacrificing loyalty to Christ rather than to
dogma or the performance of rites. It seems likely, as Bataillon suggests, that the recurrent Pauline metaphor of the
Body and the Head, a kind of *Leitmotif* in the key chapters
of the book, reflects the deep impression Colet's preaching
on Saint Paul had made on Erasmus.[5]

And so, perhaps, do the title and the framework he chose
for his treatise. "Put on the armor of God," the Apostle had
written the Ephesians. Christian life was a battle that required the shield of faith, the helmet of salvation, and the
sword of the Spirit, which is the word of God. But not everyone could take up the whole *gladium Spiritus* in its ponderous
Vulgate version, even though every Christian was, perforce,
a *miles* sworn to battle the world, the flesh, and the Devil.
What he needed was a kind of all-occasions weapon, something portable, practical, and concrete enough to give real
meaning to the Scriptural metaphor. Hence, an *enchiridion*,
a poniard, for this soldier of Christ. The word also had the
double appropriateness of meaning "handbook"—the *Man-
uel of a Christian Knyght*, the first English translator called
it; Erasmus, however, chose to stress the militant imagery. It
was a *pugiunculus*, a dagger; a *gladiolus*, small blade, not too
cumbersome to keep handy or too ineffectual to do any good.
If people thought it necessary to arm themselves physically

against the danger of highwaymen, was it not even more essential to arm the mind and spirit to cope with the real difficulties of everyday Christian living?

Inferentially, at least, the book began as a guidebook for a specific person. The opening and closing passages seem to be vestigial traces of what may have begun simply as a rather lengthy letter which later was expanded into the treatise we have now. The recipient, perhaps, was one John de Trazegnies, a dissolute soldier who had a wife of "extraordinary piety," but who cordially disliked the clergy in general— *uno me excepto,* according to Erasmus.[6] The wife had prevailed upon Erasmus to set down some notes that would restore to her husband some sense of religion, but he began them with the conventionally diplomatic pretext that the rake himself was eager to flee from the fleshpots of Egypt. Started at the castle of Tournehem, where the author and others had been driven to escape the plague at Paris, the treatise was completed at St. Omer in 1501 and afterward worked up for publication in Louvain in 1503, as part of his *Lucubratiunculae.* [7]

In its immediate reformatory purpose, apparently, the *Enchiridion* had no spectacular success. Fourteen years after its publication, Erasmus wrote to a "Master John," generally assumed to be the original recipient of the notes, to point out that the book was being widely read and improving many people; therefore "we"—with gentle tact—ought not allow a book one of "us" wrote for the sake of the other to do "us" no good at all.[8] A year later he was being more candid: in a letter to Abbot Volz he complained that the man he did the work for in the first place was, if anything, more deeply immersed in worldliness than ever.[9] We must assume, however, that neither *Magister Joannus* nor his anxiously pious wife had more than an incidental importance in the birth of the *Enchiridion.* Sooner or later Erasmus was bound to have his say on the matters closest to his heart, and the

manual ostensibly turned out for an affable debauchee became the occasion of his first full, and in some ways best,
formulation of the message intended for all Christendom, the
same message he was to repeat—often in more playful and
ironic guise—in the *Praise of Folly* and numerous colloquies.

What he wanted to do, as he told Colet shortly after its
publication, was not to show off his own cleverness and
eloquence, but to offer a corrective for what he had come
to see as the common error of all those who were turning
religion into an empty ceremonialism almost worse than that
of the Jews, and becoming profoundly indifferent to everything truly relevant to Christian piety.[10] Years later, it seems,
he was almost aghast at his own temerity in running so directly counter, as he thought, to the times: "In Enchiridion
quantum ausus sum a saeculo nostro dissentire nullius auc-
toritate deterritus!"[11] Actually, of course, he had sounded a
kind of ground bass already muttering in his times. Within
two decades the reformers of the more extreme left were
composing variations that Erasmus himself deplored; while,
changing the metaphor, the Counter Reformation on the
right sourly accused him of laying the eggs Luther had
hatched.

There was a good deal, certainly, that the dissidents could
relish: his rough handling of the brisk profiteering in the
Church, his gibes at scholastic theologians, his suggestion
that the monastic life was not necessarily a second baptism,
or even Christian, his insistence that men might better imitate the lives of saints than burn candles to them or gape at
one of their soiled handkerchiefs. More importantly, the
Enchiridion presented Erasmus' vision of an inward religion,
a Christianity based upon the ethical implications of "the
philosophy of Christ" and thus most likely to produce a
world in which reason and the will of God prevailed. It
underlined his conviction that any belief without practical
content is meaningless. It insisted upon a return, theologi-

cally, to a kind of Christian primitivism, placing the center of
gravity in the sources, *divinae Scripturae fontes*,[12] rather
than in the trifling subtleties of argument invented by the
professionals. And the soundest preparation for drinking at
these pure fountains was a solid grounding in classical literature, especially Plato, along with the early Fathers—Jerome,
Origen, Augustine, Ambrose.

Renaissance and Reformation, Preserved Smith has observed, were "fundamentally two branches of the same movement,"[13] but the two branches resist the application of any
convenient labels. We ordinarily tag the Renaissance as an
aristocratic movement and therefore "conservative"; the
Reformation as a popular one, and therefore "liberal." But if
Erasmus was later to be shocked by the "radicalism" of
Luther's rejection of the sacramental system of the Church,
Luther was himself to be no less appalled by the "liberalism"
of Erasmus. The word "protestantism" itself, as J. W. Allen
has reminded us, has its awkwardness: if we identify it with

> a claim to liberty for the individual to reach his own
> conclusions about religion in his own way and express
> them freely without interference, who, in the sixteenth
> century, was a Protestant? . . . certainly Calvin was not
> a Protestant, nor Beza nor Knox nor Whitgift. Luther
> had leanings to Protestantism, but finally went over to
> the other side.[14]

And Erasmus, one might add, the conservative who remained
in the Church, was in this sense closer to Protestantism than
those who are now assigned the mantle.

It is not surprising that the *Enchiridion,* the product of a
mind involved in both branches of the movement, should em-
body a good deal of this significant—and troublesome—
bifurcation. To the twentieth-century reader it is a matter of
interest, historical and academic; in the sixteenth century,
however, it was much more. Erasmus said, or implied, both
too much and too little; and disenchantment began to devel-

op on the left as well as the right. By the middle twenties of the century a correspondent at the College of Louvain, a Catholic stronghold, was telling Erasmus that the professors there were trying to keep his works, especially the *Enchiridion,* out of the hands of students.[15] And, on the other side, Luther decided even earlier that Erasmus was doing little to "promote the cause of Christ and God's grace" because he seemed to think "human considerations have an absolute preponderance over divine."[16] By 1525 the German could dismiss the great humanist as a trivial stylist whose much-heralded piece on free will, *De Libero Arbitrio,* was like so much dung, resplendently packaged in gold and silver. "Whenever I pray," he wrote later on, "I pray for a curse upon Erasmus."[17]

All this after beginning in warm admiration. It was not, certainly, that Erasmus had altered his position after 1503. Rather, one must suppose many readers of the *Enchiridion* were so eager to see Rome scorched that they ignored the less obvious sparks which could later sting Wittenberg. What they were slow to do, apparently, was apply to their reading of Erasmus' book the advice it contained on how to read any book. Preeminently, of course, Erasmus was concerned with the understanding of Scripture; but all literature of any consequence, he assured his audience, communicates at two levels. It has a surface, or literal, meaning and a *mysterium,* or hidden one. Like everything else in this dualistic universe, books, then, have their "flesh" and "spirit." Addressing readers for whom "new" criticism had not yet turned such advice into banality, he urged his point explicitly and with illustrations: the childish mind stops with literalization, the adult mind probes through the flesh for the spirit. "As a matter of fact," he remarked, "a poetic tale read allegorically may perhaps be more fruitful than an account from the sacred books where you content yourself with only the rind."[18]

One may suggest, then, that the militant reformers found the rind of the *Enchiridion* succulent enough to make them a little tardy about inspecting what it covered. But the analogy cannot be pressed too hard. In the constitution of the *Enchiridion* spirit and flesh are more consubstantial than antithetical; Erasmus the humanist and Erasmus the reformer were two sides of the same coin. The difficulty lay in this very identity of values, which for Erasmus was so natural and matter-of-course. When he advanced the claims of the spirit against the letter and flesh of sacramentalism and attendance at mass, no one, except those who stood to profit from the exploitation of letter and flesh, could quarrel with his championship of the general principle of inwardness, his insistence that in the Christian experience something had to happen to a man's heart and mind. But what? And how was it to come about? Once having swallowed the skin of the *Enchiridion's* teaching, those with a moderately good nose for dogma scented something at variance with the pure odor of sanctity.

For one thing, there was the very patent assumption of the importance of mind. Naturally, the very fact that Erasmus had formulated a working set of rules for the achievement of the good life suggested a certain confidence in man's rational powers; indeed, the inward reform he advocated has struck some present-day critics as being less moral than mental. To Erasmus the distinction would have seemed more verbal than real, and the case he makes for the interdependence—the virtual integrity—of these two aspects of inwardness suggests a thinker not only, as Bainton has pointed out, much more subversive of medieval Catholicism than was Luther,[19] but equally subversive of some of the Reformation's own favorite orthodoxies.

Early in the treatise his attitude begins to take shape for the reader. The Christian soldier, he says, needs two special weapons: prayer and knowledge. *Precatio* intercedes and establishes communication with God; let us concede it the greater potency. Still, *scientia* puts the intellect in touch with salutary ideas, suggests what we should pray for; neither weapon is very effective without the other. Knowledge and understanding nourish faith and the more transcendental fervencies that translate themselves into prayer.

There is no valid reason, I think, to question the genuineness of Erasmus' own faith or the sincerity of his belief in the efficacy of prayer. Nevertheless, one detects throughout most of the *Enchiridion* a concern for the nourishment itself that would have disquieted those whose own enthusiasms were more revelational. Regeneration, for Erasmus, is a process, not a seizure or a private apocalypse. You begin, he tells his reader, with the Socratic injunction, "Know yourself." This is the chief point of wisdom, and it is not easy. You must know, first of all, that well-domesticated enemy, your carnal inheritance from old Adam. You must know that your breast is like a factious commonwealth, where only the firm control of reason prevents the anarchy of passion. You must know the real meaning of the terms *flesh* and *spirit;* how else can you follow Paul's exhortation to die to the one and live in the other?

What else but this kind of understanding, after all, will prick the quasi-superstition currently passing for Christianity into an awareness that hanging a cross around one's neck is an absurdity without the imitation of Christ in one's living? A religion frozen in ritual and ceremony is as flesh-bound in its own way as lechery or gluttony. And more dangerous, actually, since what was intended originally to support and feed "infants in Christ" becomes identified with piety itself. Thus all Christendom suffers from a case of arrested development palming itself off as holiness, and the spirit starves because Christians scarcely know what spirit means.

What it means here, clearly, is a day-by-day working out of the pattern of New Testament behavior, the practical application of the Sermon on the Mount. By the time he reaches Rule Six, Erasmus is ready to make a kind of Socratic-Aristotelian equation of virtue with a habit of the will based upon sound knowledge. A man can live like a Christian only when he has thoroughly learned the real Christian values, through learning them loved them, and through loving them cultivated them—consciously, voluntarily, and for their own sake. He can live like a Christian only when he is spiritually adult enough to know what is at stake: the stubborn, and often galling, application of principles that go against every natural instinct and affront every canon of "realism" and "commonsense." One can see the climactic paradox of the *Praise of Folly* already gestating in the earlier work. The Christian must grow up into madness, into the splendid folly of the saints. "He is happily a fool who is wise in Christ, miserably a fool who doesn't know Him."[20]

This, at least, is the ideal that Erasmus offers as the goal of the finest spirits. Obviously, the common run of men are not going to set much store by such renunciation and self-discipline—and the spiritual "common run," he knows, will embrace a good many princes and nobles, both secular and churchly. Granting, however, that saintly asceticism is the magnificent idiosyncracy of the few, we need not scorn the second best which at least looks in that direction. Ordinary moral decency, after all, makes a better groundwork for the heroic virtues than does depravity, and even without the deepest sense of what they owe Christ, Christians might reasonably be expected to live as uprightly as, say, the many pagans who were good simply because they considered virtue more compatible than vice with their own humanity.

In the miscellany of rules concluding the book, the importance Erasmus was willing to assign to rational self-government becomes more explicit; he spells out techniques and procedures:

> If you are inflamed by lust, acknowledge your weakness and deny yourself somewhat more, even of lawful pleasures; assign yourself an additional number of chaste and moral duties. If you are enticed by greed or avarice, increase your charitable donations. If you are attracted by empty fame, humble yourself that much more in every respect.[21]

By the practice of conscious asceticism one toughens his moral fiber and converts his own share in original sin into a serviceable, if unwilling, sparring partner. For Erasmus, clearly, moral tone must at least be the condition of the Christian life, if not its justification; and the road to both cannot be wholly closed to human effort. God intended us to be the consorts of angels, of course; we should pray for this ultimate in felicity. But in the meantime we can do something by keeping in mind that we are men, not beasts—a fact Erasmus saw only as a challenge, not a predicament.

The immediate need, then, is not so much the sudden illumination of divine grace as a clear-sighted understanding of sin's profits and losses, an understanding sharpened, happily, by a sufficient sense of the ludicrous and incongruous. Grace will descend most readily where there is a place for it; one infers from the *Enchiridion* that the amount available to the slack, the stupid, and the humorless is not likely to be abundant. Let a fornicating priest begin, we are told, by at least reminding himself of the shocking indecorum of becoming "one body and one spirit with God—and one body with a tart." Let an elderly lecher look in the mirror and receive the instruction from age that he should have received from reason. Let the hot-tempered remember that the difference between an enraged man and a madman is the difference between temporary and chronic insanity. Let the

vengeful see that evening a score is more than unChristian;
it is unintelligent.

> For what will be the eventual result of these reciprocal
> injuries if everyone hastens to retaliate in kind for his
> own grievance? Enemies multiply on all sides, the
> grievance is exacerbated, and the longer it lasts, the
> more incurable it is. . . . Through vengeance . . . that
> very injury which you wish to ward off recoils upon
> yourself, and not without usurious interest on the
> capital.[22]

Such a program for ethical rejuvenation obviously assigns
a relatively minor role to both dogma and mysticism. His
title notwithstanding, the critics of Erasmus found reason to
suspect that the *pietas* he espoused was too independent of
doctrine to be specifically Christian, that he had never really
slammed the door to salvation on heretics, or even pagans.

This is not to say, as Luther eventually did, that the *Enchiridion* takes as its model Plato rather than Christ. However, working from the postulate that "any truth you come
upon at any place is Christ's," Erasmus could drink with apparently impartial zest from either Jordan or the springs of
Helicon, blending the *Timaeus* with *Corinthians*, Hesiod
with Matthew, even Terence with *Isaiah*. Years later a character in his colloquy "The Godly Feast" was to epitomize
this attitude in a famous passage on the virtuous ancients:
"And so, when I read such things of such men, I can hardly
help exclaiming, 'Saint Socrates, pray for us!' "[23]

"Sancte Socrates, ora pro nobis!" Such an invocation was
blasphemous nonsense to Luther, who in an equally characteristic passage in *Bondage of the Will* sounded the harsher
note of the Reformers' orthodoxy. He would grant that certain of the ancients—Cicero, for example—had surpassed
Christians in talent, in hard work, even in earnestness. But
none of these qualities, however admirable, could win them
grace; though they pursued truth with all their heart, not one

of them reached it. Their virtue was born in pride. Because they did nothing for the glory of God, but for themselves, their hearts were corrupt and impious. They were "never less upright and more vile than when they shone in their highest virtues."[24]

In the generous admiration of Erasmus for what even pagans could do, and the fierce certainty of Luther as to what they, or any other man, could not do, we have a distillation of the central debate of the Renaissance involving the doctrine of man. To the question "What shall I do to be saved?" Luther's answer was grimly unequivocal: Nothing. Nothing that will affect your fate. Indeed, any action of yours, however good it seems, will be no more than sin if not founded on faith. Even to *think* that you can make the smallest contribution to your own salvation is to invite damnation. True, a man may act spontaneously and voluntarily, but he is powerless to alter, restrain, or eliminate this volition in his own strength. Since either God or Satan dictates to it, man's will is like a beast standing between two riders.

"If God rides, it wills and goes where God wills. . . . If Satan rides, it wills and goes where Satan wills. Nor may it choose to which rider it will run, or which it will seek. . . ."[25]

To Luther and the other radical Reformers it was clear that Satan had mounted Cato, Socrates, Cicero, and their company, and, in the guise of virtuous self-sufficiency, spurred them straight into hell. At the antipodes stood Italian humanism; Pico maintained that we are "constrained by no limits" and can transform ourselves into either brutes or divinities, in accordance with our own free will; that we can, by "emulating the Cherubic way of life on earth, by taming the impulses of our passions with moral science, by dispelling the darkness of reason with dialectic, and by, so to speak, washing away the filth of ignorance and vice, cleanse our

soul, so that her passions may not rave at random or her
reason through heedlessness ever be deranged."[26] And Ficino
argued that the human intellect partook of the "highest form
of perfection," and was, "after perfection itself, in the highest
degree perfect."[27]

In the one camp human mind and will were given so much
that divine grace itself began to seem superfluous; in the
other, they were conceded little or nothing in order that God
should be everything. The will was impotent and corrupt, and
Reason, in Luther's famous pejorative, was a whore. To many
of the Evangelicals the *Enchiridion* may very well have read
like a guidebook to pandering. More accurately, however, it
reveals Erasmus' wary distaste for all such overwhelming
simplicities of conviction, whether from the North or the
South. He accepted the doctrine of the Fall and of man's corrupted nature, but credited him with a thirst for some nobler
state. He knew reason was far from perfect and that, to com-
pound the hazards, Scripture was often obscure and recon-
dite. He knew that the fullest self-knowledge, unattainable
even to his beloved Saint Paul, would remain an impossible
goal, but that the very effort of reaching for it had its own
therapy. He was aware that goodness itself, or what customarily passed for it, could lead to enormities of bigotry
and harshness, whereas a man's very frailties could be made
to serve as catalysts of regeneration. Without dismissing the
fact of human capacity for sin, he insisted upon making a distinction between the inclination and the sin itself.

In his *Diatribe on Free Will* he was to make more explicit
his position, a stand characteristically midway between the
more or less pagan humanism of the Italians and the iron
pessimism of the Reformation. Will, inspired by divine grace,
has its own role to play: it can turn toward the course that
leads to salvation, or away from it. The two causes work together and, inferentially, the horse has some measure of
choice as to its rider. The inexorable determination of the

Lutheran or the Calvinist made all human effort foolish and God a monster. Erasmus, too, was eager to justify the ways of God to man, and his sense of human dignity and potentiality rebelled against a concept of Deity that stultified all human merit and reduced every effort, however pious, to an act of sin. The Christianity Erasmus was championing in the *Enchiridion* and elsewhere—though certainly not "rational" in the sense of holding reason to be the sole guide to religious truth—clearly embodied his own preference for the simple and the reasonable. It predicated a God too much the Christian Humanist to nullify whatever men could do to be humanly Christian.

Doctrinally, of course, he was eating his cake and having it; practically, he knew that the balanced view became, in the actual logistics of Christian warfare, a kind of balancing act. The trick, as he saw it in the *Diatribe*, was to avoid the "Scylla of pride" without falling into the "Charybdis of despair." One thinks of Newman, who, more than three centuries later, could argue eloquently for intellectual excellence as an end in itself, who conceded it the capacity to produce behavior something like the religious, but who regretfully acknowledged that this apparent ally could very well become an out-and-out foe to Christian faith because it tended to substitute confident self-mastery for humility and despairing awareness of human corruption. What Newman outlined in *The Idea of a University* was not, to be sure, the balancing act between pride and despair, but the cultivation of the best in our nature while we resolutely remind ourself of the worst in it. One is left with a sense of the conflicting claims of two very nearly incompatible blessings; one escapes Scylla only by the saving plunge into Charybdis.

Newman was a better Catholic than Erasmus. And so, in this sense, was Luther, who "knew" from early youth that he deserved condemnation and hell, who was subject to acute feelings of depression as well as to moments of high exalta-

tion, and who concluded from these moments of agonized
fear that man's nature was so corrupt that it could be remade
only through the undeserved miracle of divine forgiveness.
Out of his subjective conviction of a desperate situation grew
his belief in desperate remedies, and his contempt for the
semi-Pelagianism of Erasmus. The humanist seemed far too
much at ease in Zion: "you who, I dare say, never dropped
a tear or uttered a sigh for the doctrine of Christ in your
life!"[28]

No doubt he was right. The *Enchiridion* never strikes one
as the cry of an anguished heart. It is no flippancy to suggest
that, for Erasmus, the active waging of Christian battle would
leave little time for tears and sighs. It needed vigor of mind
more than intensity of feeling. *Cogita* and *existima* are his
favorite imperatives, not *lacrima* or *miserere*, or even *exsulta*.
If the Christianity outlined here is "classical," as it is sometimes described, not the least of its classical qualities is this
equable middle register of emotional pitch, skirting the rich
enthusiasms of either bass or treble. William James' remark
about the Hellenic temperament seems equally appropriate
to Erasmus: like the Greeks he so much admired, he had not
discovered that "the enduring emphasis, so far as this world
goes, may be laid on its pain and failure"; and if, as James
thought, the "completest religions" are those in which the
pessimistic elements are most fully developed, then Erasmus
offers something less. It is not so much that he empties his
world of extremities as that he consciously translates into
viable material for thought what, for a less classical temperament, could unconsciously be made to feed a pathological
melancholy. "I should say," he remarks at the end of his
chapter "Against Pride," "that two things above all will ward
off arrogance: one, keeping in mind just what you are, in
yourself—repugnant when you enter life, a bubble throughout the course of it, worm's meat when you leave it—and,
two, remembering what Christ became for your sake."[29]

The least one can say is that, for a Luther, the injunction to "remember" or "keep in mind" such dramatic incongruities might well seem inadequate, if not superfluous. To those who experience their religion in nerve centers and the pit of the stomach, this would imply a certain frugality of emotional response. Erasmus may have thought of the right things, but he seemed not to have felt the right way when he thought them.

It is possible that this conspicuous lack of anguish may serve to disqualify Erasmus as one to speak very convincingly to at least a certain segment of the modern mind. The most recent translators of Luther's treatise on the will, for example, dismiss the humanist on two grounds: one, his indifference to dogma and, two, his offering only a "barren moralism,"[30] an "eviscerated Christianity . . . without Christ at the deepest level," one which demonstrates "cool calculation" rather than "burning conviction."[31] Inferentially, the second is the cause of the first. If Erasmus had really sensed the corruption of human will and the blindness of reason, he would not have tried to have the best of both worlds in a doctrinal sense. He would not have treated the religious experience as a cooperative enterprise between man and divine grace, "as if God exists for man's convenience, rather than man for God's glory."[32]

Obviously, these strictures reveal at least as much about the premises of the critics themselves as about Erasmus; one may share their distaste for Erasmus' coolness, if not their particular theological bias. A considerable portion of the most highly regarded literature of the past half century suggests that the enduring emphasis, so far as this world goes— and so far as current taste is concerned—had indeed better be on its pain and failure. Insofar as he cares a fig what anybody says or thinks about the nature and condition of man, today's reader seems to respond more warmly to a description of his syndrome than to a moderately confident assessment of his possibilities. The most tolerable whistle is one patently sounded in the dark.

It is not unlikely, of course, that a fair amount of the alienation and anguish the twentieth-century intellectual takes as his hallmark may be too metaphysical to cause much loss of sleep or appetite. One is reminded of Dr. Johnson's reply to Boswell, who had complained of being much disturbed by the question of Liberty and Necessity: "I hoped you had got rid of all this hypocrisy of misery. . . . I love every part about you but your affectation of distress." An abstracted and apotheosized emotion goes only a very little way toward depressing the mind, and even the most excited existentialist may respond less poignantly, say, to his being cosmically condemned to freedom than academically condemned to another year as assistant professor.

As Pascal once observed, few speak humbly of humility or doubtingly of skepticism. And he might have added: or hopelessly of despair. Human nature being what it is, the Scylla and Charybdis of Erasmus sometimes have a way of becoming indistinguishable; a man may publicly eat his heart out with something of the ambivalence of motive Cicero observed in the philosophers who, having written their books on the emptiness of reputation, signed their names to them. It seems a favorite romanticism—taking some liberty with Lovejoy's taxonomy—of our own century to identify most of reality with the abyss. To experience in a large, transcendental way some of Pascal's celebrated vertigo is thus the certificate of spiritual prestige, and sackcloth becomes the affectation of *hubris*.

Admittedly, then, the Erasmian version of religious experience may very well seem pallid to tastes seeking either a more Gothic richness at the subliminal level of religious consciousness or a more towering superstructure of dogma which, to return to Jamesian phraseology, is merely the translation of that subliminal text into another tongue. Wagnerians and Mahlerites are not likely to become much addicted to Haydn. Still, the classical virtues are no less real for being of a different order, and Erasmus cannot very sensibly be dismissed for not doing what he would have considered either trivial or impertinent. Assuming, as most critics do, that in his private spiritual experience he had never felt himself teetering on the edge of a void, it is just as probable that had he done so it would not have occurred to him that he should turn his writing into a means of measuring his nausea. Like any classicist, he concerned himself with the generally valid, not the personal and idiosyncratic. The real value of the inwardness he was advocating lay not merely in the individual justification of its possessor, either by faith or by works, but in the attendant social expression, a beneficent contagion that could sweeten the relationships of the whole human community. Significantly, references in the *Enchiridion* to either hope of heaven or threat of hell are relatively infrequent; when they do occur they sound almost by-the-way. For Erasmus, Christianity's center of gravity lay in an area accessible to human understanding and human effort, and perhaps we call attention to the defect of his qualities when we note that the claims Arnold later made for culture differ in almost no essential characteristic from those Erasmus made for the Philosophy of Christ: the perfection of human nature in the balanced serenity of sweetness and light.

The truth of an idea, then, lay in what happened to it— happened to it in the sense, that is, of making reason and the Will of God prevail, of encouraging what Arnold was to call in *Culture and Anarchy* "the growth and predominance of our humanity proper, as distinguished from our animality." Truth in this sense could get along with a minimum of dogma, whether of the Right from Rome or the Left from Wittenberg. As Preserved Smith has pointed out, when Erasmus and Luther argued the freedom of the will, what was a matter of life and death to Luther was little more than an interesting subject of conversation to Erasmus.[33] Near the end of his life he was still shrugging it aside as a matter of peripheral importance: "a thorny question which it profits little to debate; let us leave it to professed theologians."[34] He suspected, indeed, that the professionals liked to multiply and sharpen the thorns to their own advantage, keeping the untutored layman troubled by difficulties and obscurities when everything central to true piety, the "Philosophy of Christ," could be made plain and easy to every man.[35]

The unknowable, that is, could be deferred until the Day of Judgment. Trinity and vicarious atonement, predestination and election—all knowledge here remained verbal, but men at odds with one another in matters of creed could still demonstrate the real truth of Christ in their deeds. When Erasmus defended Luther it was on the ground that he differed from the Church in no *essential* point of doctrine and that his life was blameless.[36] The fact that men could wrangle endlessly over the meaning of Scripture was evidence enough that Scripture was often ambiguous and obscure, even for the sharpest and best-trained minds; it followed then, as Bainton has put it, that the amount of belief necessary for salvation could not exceed the comprehension of the most obtuse.[37] The rudest understanding, on the other hand, could grasp the practical import of the Sermon on the Mount; heretical beliefs were irrelevant to the imitation of Christ.

It is a frequently remarked irony that Luther, who would allow reason only light to see that it was blind, would yet argue fiercely, and along scholastic lines, about matters of faith, whereas the Erasmus identified with rationalism insisted upon intellectual humility toward unsolvable problems. His position reminds us of the fideism of Montaigne, who could firmly put faith outside the bounds of rational understanding and still say he was bound to serve nothing but reason. Certainly Erasmus supposed he was serving God as well, but he had a mind too complicated for furious certitudes, too modest to suppose that in his every insight he was realizing a share of the final promise made to Moses that he would see God's backside. It took a Luther to say that "through enlightening of the Holy Ghost, the special gift of God, one enjoys complete certainty in judging of and deciding between the doctrines and opinions of all men as they affect oneself and one's own personal salvation."[38]

Obviously, between moments of mystical revelation on the one hand and periods of intellectualizing those moments on the other, men spend most of their waking hours not much concerned with either. Whatever a person may suppose he thinks about the inefficacy of reason, his philosophic stance is not likely to deter him from making a good many decisions between breakfast and dinner; and one doubts that Luther was much exercised about the impotence of will when he threw his weight behind the princes in the Peasants' Revolt. Experience, as Johnson knew, can make logic an impertinence: "Sir, we *know* our will is free, and *there's* an end on't."

The scope and matter of the *Enchiridion* suggest essentially the same restriction of interest to the measurably valid as the Doctor's crotchety pronouncement. The really significant Christian campaigning goes on at a level of immediate and concrete exigency where debates over supernal strategy, it seemed to Erasmus, have little practical bearing. For every combatant it resolves itself into a series of day-by-day tussles, limited and specific, with his unregenerate self. It is a matter of gradually—and strenuously—achieving a quality of mature desire, of growing up to his humanity proper through a process of renunciation and self-discipline, while every day his own share in the first Adam is reminding him of the claims of his animality. Piety without a resisting object is meaningless, and the only goodness one can intelligibly talk about is the kind men have to grope for in a context of recalcitrant flesh and worldly values. When Erasmus insisted upon intelligent and enlightened moral effort, he did not suppose that men would lift themselves into heaven by their bootstraps, but neither did he suppose that a Christian ethic treated as a kind of inevitable serendipity of faith—faith in the "right" dogmas or in the right observances—would ever be much more than the splendid eccentricity of a few. Once men have assumed that goodness and salvation depend entirely on a will other than their own, they are likely to infer either that moral effort is pointless or that the Holy Ghost has authorized every enormity that passionate conviction suggests. It is within the scope of each Christian soldier to act here and now as a member of that Body of which Christ is Head, but not to fractionize that Body in demonstrating that God's intentions for populating the New Jerusalem are identical with his own.

Luther upbraided Erasmus for seeming unduly concerned about "this carnal peace and quiet" rather than "faith, conscience, salvation, the Word of God, the glory of Christ, and God himself." Better, he continued sternly, to have tumult, destruction of the world itself than to lose God.[39]

This is the *either-or* of zealotry and passion. Erasmus, like the reasonable and cultivated men of all ages, rejected both the simplicity and the intensity which could imagine God's glory best served by the destruction of God's creatures. "Of what use," asks the *Enchiridion*, "are the terms of discord where unity is everything?" And a little later: "A Christian, therefore, is commanded to compete with all men only in love, gentleness, and good deeds, and to willingly give over contention, hatred, slander, insults, and injury. . . ."[40]

Such things, of course, most men have never willingly given over for any considerable length of time, and the strident *either-or's* from both Inquisition and Reformation effectually drowned out the lower-keyed, and somehow more difficult, voice of Erasmus. Protestantism today, it has been

INTRODUCTION

said, is more Erasmian than Lutheran because of its "doc-trinal indifferentism."[41] A real test, however, would demand something more positive: a pervasive awareness that truth must be sought in humility, a readiness to forgo the reassuring thrill of absolutes.

The "tragic defect" of Erasmus, according to Huizinga, was his inability, or unwillingness, to draw "ultimate conclusions."[42] One wonders, though, as Erasmus must have wondered, if the world has not had a plethora of "ultimate conclusions" which make men willing to kill and die, but never to be reasonable. This *was* his ultimate conclusion, and of course it lacks the compelling intensity of passion that produced a More or a Tyndale, a Servetus or a Savonarola. Like Montaigne, Erasmus would follow no cause into the fire. However, men willing to be burned for causes have frequently been willing to burn others. For an Erasmus, the only valid goal of the Christian faith was one which reciprocal martyrdoms would not reach: a world in which men "wish for good, pray for good, act for good to all men" on the ground that they are all "mutual members of one another."

We could do much worse, it seems, and ordinarily we do.

RAYMOND HIMELICK

THE

ENCHIRIDION

OF ERASMUS

Prefatory Enjoinder

AGERLY YOU HAVE petitioned me, dearest brother in the Lord, to prescribe in a concise fashion some method of living which might help you achieve a character acceptable to Christ. You say that for some time now you have been tiring of the life of the court, that you are casting about for whatever means you can find of fleeing Egypt with all its vices and pleasures and, under the guidance of a Moses, successfully preparing for the path of righteousness.

Your salutary design makes me all the more happy because I am so fond of you; I trust that He who served to inspire it in you will speed and carry it forward, even without my help. Nevertheless, I am glad to comply with your request, partly because you are such a dear friend and partly because you are asking for such good things. But you must also exert yourself, lest you seem to have asked my aid without a real reason, or I to have complied with your wishes without real results. Rather, let us join in asking the blessed spirit of Jesus, not only to furnish me with sound advice when I write, but to make that advice of real service to you.

TWO

In This Life One Must Be on Guard

IN THE FIRST place, you should continually bear in mind that mortal life is nothing but a kind of perpetual warfare—as Job testifies,[1] a soldier both widely experienced and consistently invincible—and very much deceived are the general run of men, whose minds this mountebank of a world captivates with alluring pleasures, who take unseasonable furloughs as if the fighting were already over and they were not living in a most hazardous peace.

It is strange to see how confidently they live, how soddenly they sleep—now on the one side, now on the other—while we are being assaulted without letup by such ironshod hordes of vices, ambushed by so many stratagems, beset by so many snares! Just look about you: the vilest demons sleeplessly watch for your ruin, and they are equipped with a thousand tricks and devices for doing us harm. From aloft they strive to wound our souls with fiery and deadly missiles, steeped in venom and every bit as unerring as even the dart of a Hercules or a Cephalus[2] unless they are intercepted by the impenetrable shield of faith. Again, to the right and to the left, in van and rear, this world which, in the words of John, is wholly bent on mischief,[3] assails us. For that reason it was both hostile and abhorrent to Christ.

Nor is there any cut and dried method of attack. Sometimes storming us in open warfare, so to speak, by means of adversity the foe batters the walls of the mind with heavy ram. At other times he provokes us to defection with resounding but empty promises. Yet again, covertly and by secret maneuvers, he creeps up to catch us unaware among the careless and the negligent. And, last of all, that hellishly slippery serpent, the first destroyer of our peace—now concealed in the green grass, now lurking in hundredfold coils in those caverns of his[4]—never ceases to lie in ambush in the heel of woman, whom he once corrupted. Keep in mind that "woman" is man's sensual part: she is our Eve, through whom that wiliest of serpents lures our passions into deadly pleasures.

Then, as if so many enemies threatening us on all sides were not enough, within the most private recesses of our consciousness we carry a foe more intimate, more domesticated; and just as nothing in us is more secret, so nothing can be more dangerous. This is that ancient and earthy Adam, in companionable familiarity more than a citizen, in his actions worse than an enemy. We can neither wall him out nor drive him from our camp. This fellow we must watch with a hundred eyes or he may, perhaps, throw God's citadel open to the spirits of hell.

Therefore, since we are all engaged in such formidable and taxing warfare and have enemies so numerous, so committed to our destruction, so zealous, so vigilant, so well-armed, so treacherous, so skillful, are we not of dubious sanity if we, on our part, do not arm ourselves, stand on guard, and hold all things suspect? But just as if conditions were absolutely tranquil, we snore away flat on our backs; we do nothing, we enjoy ourselves and, as they say, idly look after our skins,[5] as though this life of ours were not a war, but a Greek drinking bout. In place of tents and camps, we wallow about in bed; in place of tough armor we are bedecked with roses and the voluptuous charms of Adonis; in place of military exercise we abandon ourselves to debauchery and sloth; in place of warlike weapons we fondle the impotent lute.

As if this peace of ours were not actually the most shameful kind of war, for surely a man who has come to terms with his vices has violated the covenant he made with God at his baptism. You lunatic! You cry "Peace! Peace!" when you have God as your enemy, who alone is peace and the author of peace.[6] He himself refutes you in the words of His glorious prophet: "There is no peace for the wicked."[7] For there is no other condition of peace with Him except to wage war upon our sins with all our might and deepest loathing, as long as we shall serve in this fortress of the body. Otherwise—if we compromise with those sins—we shall have Him who is the only one capable of doing good for us as an ally and destroying us as a foe twice our adversary: not only because we take our stand with those things incompatible with God (for how can light be compatible with darkness?),[8] but because we have ungratefully failed to keep faith with Him and impiously dissolved a pact we made with the holiest of ceremonies.

Do you not know, you soldier of Christ, that when you were admitted to the mysteries of the life-giving fountain you gave your name to Christ, your Commander, to whom you owe your life twice over, seeing that He both gave it and restored it to you, and to whom you owe more than you yourself can repay? Do you not remember that when you were bound with His sacraments, as with holy gifts, you swore allegiance in express terms to so blessed a Leader and exposed your head to His wrath if you did not stand by the agreement?

What was the use of having the sign of the Cross outlined on your forehead unless you were to live by it and campaign under His standard? What point in being sprinkled with holy oil unless you were to wage unremitting war upon your vices? When some man betrays his prince, how shameful we consider him! What a general anathematizing from practically the whole human race! Then why do you make a joke of Christ, neither deterred by fear of Him (although He is God) nor prevented by love (although for your sake He was made man)? Seeing that you make a show of His name, you should be mindful of what you have promised Him. Why do you cravenly go over to the adversary, from whom He once redeemed you with the ransom of His blood?[9] Why, as a two-time deserter, do you serve in the camp of the enemy? With what kind of effrontery do you dare to raise hostile standards against your King, who offered His life for you? As He has said, whoever does not stand with Him stands against Him; and whoever does not serve in His company is a straggler.[10]

Moreover, you who serve the world not only serve in a foul cause but for miserable pay. Would you like to hear what that pay is? Well, Paul, the standard bearer of Christian forces, tells you: "The wage of sin," he says, "is death."[11] Now, who would undertake even some glamorous military service which was sure to result in physical death? Are you, then, going to accept as your pay so foul a death of the soul?

In those insane wars man wages against man either because of grinding necessity or animal fury, do you not see that whenever the prospect of rich loot or the dreaded cruelty of a foe who is victorious or the shame of being taunted with cowardice or the desire for praise has kindled the spirits of the soldiery, with what lusty zeal they perform any operation, how cheap they hold their lives, with what abandon they hurl themselves upon their enemies? And what trifling reward, I ask you, do these wretched fellows seek at such risk and with such fierceness? Merely that, in the uproar of battlefield or camp, they be lauded by a captain who is only a man and celebrated in some crudely flattering doggerel, or be decked out in a wreath of grass or oak leaves, or carry home a little larger purse than usual.

But we, on the other hand, are kindled neither by shame nor hope of reward, even though we have as observer of our efforts the One who will pay us off. And what rewards has our Master of the games offered to the victor? Not tripods, to be sure, or mules—such as went to Homer's Achilles or Vergil's Aeneas[12]—but things which the eye has not seen nor the ear heard, things which have never reached the heart of man.[13] These are the prizes He gives for the efforts of those who contend for them. And what then? Life, joyful and ever-lasting.

Now, in those sporting events where glory is the chief in-centive, even losers are allotted their prizes. We, however, compete in very grave and double-edged peril: we are fight-ing, not for praise but for life, and just as the best prize goes to the one who prosecutes the task enegetically, so the sever-est penalty awaits the deserter. Heaven is promised to him who fights valiantly; does not the lively courage of a noble spirit kindle at the prospect of such a happy reward, espe-cially when it is presented by that Creator who is no more able to deceive than not to be what He is?

We do everything under the eyes of an all-seeing God, we have the whole assembly of heaven as witnesses of our fight —and are we not, at the very least, stricken with shame? The One whose praise is supreme felicity will praise our courage; why do we not seek this felicity even if it costs us our lives? It is a craven heart which is not stirred by any reward, but even the most pusillanimous are customarily pricked into action by fear of danger. In their case, furthermore, even the most furious enemy can ravish only their lives and fortunes: what more could savagely victorious Achilles do to Hector?

But this adversary assaults your immortal part. Your body is not dragged around a tomb,[14] but soul and body alike are plunged into hell. In earthly warfare the ultimate disaster is that a victor's sword should part soul from body; in this other kind of warfare the soul is deprived of its very life, which is to say of God himself. It is natural for the body to perish; even if no one kills it, it is still bound to die. The worst fate, though, is for the soul to perish. With what solicitude we fend off injuries to our mortal part, with what anxiety we shudder at its dreaded extinction—because that can be seen with the physical eye. But since no one sees a dying soul, few believe in it and fewer fear it, though this death is as much more dreadful as soul is superior to body, as God is superior to soul.

Would you like me to indicate certain symptoms by which you may recognize either the sickness or death of the soul? If your stomach fails to digest properly, it will not retain its food and sooner or later you are aware of a physical illness. As bread is food for the body, so God's Word is food for the soul.[15] If this Word is distasteful to you, if it makes you sick, why doubt that your spiritual palate is ailing? If the soul does not retain the Word, if it does not pass on into its inner parts digested food for meditation, you have a clear sign of its disease.

When your knees feel weak and your feeble limbs can scarcely move, you know the body is in trouble; do you not infer soul sickness, then, when it languishes and feels squeamish over every act of piety? when it has not the strength to endure even a minor shock? when it is crushed by the loss of a little money?

After sight has left the eyes and the ears no longer hear anything and the whole body is insensate, nobody questions that the soul has left it. Well, then, if your spiritual eyes are so clouded that you do not see even the brightest light of truth, if your inward ear can not understand the voice of God, if you are utterly deficient in every spiritual awareness, do you think your soul is alive?

Suppose you see a brother being treated outrageously, but your own heart is unperturbed as long as your own welfare is not involved. Why does the soul feel nothing here? Assuredly because it is dead. Why? Because God, the life of the soul, is not there: wherever God is, love is; for God is love.[16] Otherwise, if you are a living member, how can any part of your body suffer while you not only feel no pain but are not even aware of trouble.[17]

Here is a sign even more unmistakable: suppose you have

cheated a friend, or committed adultery. Your soul has received a mortal wound, but you—far from being bothered—even rejoice as if you had turned a profit. You pride yourself on doing something shameful. Take it as a fact that your soul is dead! If the body does not feel a pin prick, it is lifeless; is the soul alive which is insensible of such a grave injury?

Suppose you hear some fellow using language that is lewd, arrogant, scurrilous, shameless, foul—railing with rabid invective at his neighbor. Do not think for a minute that that man's soul is living: a stinking corpse lies in the sepulchre of his heart, giving off a stench that infects anyone close by. Christ calls the Pharisees "whited sepulchres."[18] Why? Because they were carrying around dead souls within themselves. "Their throat is an open tomb," says the prophet-king; "with their tongues they spoke shamelessly."[19] The bodies of godly men are temples of the Holy Spirit,[20] but those of the wicked are tombs of corpses, so that the saying of the grammarians fits them very neatly: "A body resembling a tomb." The breast is the tomb, and the throat and mouth comprise the opening to it. Nor is any body bereft of soul so lifeless as the soul abandoned by God, and no physical corpse so offends the human nostrils as the stench of a soul that has been four days buried offends the nostrils of God and all the saints. Therefore, when words of death issue from your breast, a spiritual cadaver must be lying within it; for, in the words of the Gospel, when the mouth speaks from the fullness of the heart, surely it speaks the living words of God, if life—which is to say, God—is there.[21]

In another part of the Gospel, the disciples say to Christ, "Lord, where shall we go? You have the words of life."[22] Why "word of life"? Surely because they emanate from that soul who had never, even for a moment, been abandoned by the Godhead that restored us to immortal life. To the ailing body a physician gives some relief, and holy men have sometimes restored to life a body already dead. Only God, however, revives a dead soul through His singular grace and power—and not even then if that soul was in a state of death when it parted company with the body. Moreover, of corporeal death we have no consciousness, or at least very little, but of spiritual death we have an everlasting awareness; and though in other respects the soul may be as dead as can be, nevertheless, in regard to this consciousness of its own death it is somehow deathless.

Therefore, since we have to deal with a danger so extraordinary, wherefore that sluggishness, that apathy, that spiritual inertia which even fear of such great peril cannot prick into action? On the other hand, there is nothing in the magnitude of jeopardy, in the strength of the enemy forces or their cunning, which need dismay the heart and mind. If you are conscious of having a formidable adversary, remember also that you have a ready ally. Innumerable foes oppose you, but the One who stands on your side is mightier than all the rest. If God be for us, who can stand against us?[23] If He sustains us, who will overthrow us? Only accept, with your whole heart, His pledge of victory; remember that you are fighting, not an unscathed opponent, but one whom we have already discomfited, cast down, routed, and even led in triumph—but only in Christ, our Captain, by whom he will unfailingly be conquered again, and in us.

If only you see to it that you are a member of the Body, you will be able to achieve anything through the power of the Head. In yourself, of course, you are too weak; in Him, there is nothing you cannot do. The outcome of your warfare, therefore, is not in doubt, for victory by no means depends upon luck. In this business no one has ever failed to win except the fellow who did not want to. Our Defender's help has never been denied to anyone; if you take care not to be unworthy of His aid, you have already won. He will fight for you and bestow His gifts according to your deserts.

To Him who, first and uniquely free from sin,[24] quelled

sin's tyranny you must attribute every victory you win; but this victory will not come without your efforts, for He who has said, "Have faith. I have overcome the world,"[25] wants you to be confident, but not complacent. If we fight according to His example, we shall eventually be victorious through Him: therefore, you must steer a middle course between Scylla and Charybdis, shunning both the excessive reliance upon God's favor which would make you slack and careless, and the distrustful anxiety over the hazards of war, which would simultaneously deprive you of your weapons and your stomach for fighting.

THREE

Concerning the Weapons of Christian Soldiering

I CONSIDER IT especially important that in training for this campaign you plan and give very close attention to the most effective kind of weapons for meeting the enemy, so that you will always have them at hand, and that trickiest of all strategists may not fall upon you some time when you are defenseless and helpless. In your ordinary warfare a man is sometimes permitted to relax while the enemy sleeps, or while a truce is in progress. But as long as we serve in this body, we cannot get away from our weapons even by the width of a finger, as the saying goes. We must never fail to post guard over the camp, never relax our vigilance, for our adversary never sleeps. On the contrary, when he is apparently quiet, when he pretends flight or truce, that is the time he is especially busy with his tricks: never should one be more wary than when he makes a show of peace; but never is there less cause for fear than when he attacks in open battle.

So, as your first job, see to it that your mind is not defenseless. In fear of the highwayman's dagger we arm the body;

shall we not arm the mind to keep it safe? Our enemies have been equipped to destroy us; are we to be put out at having to take up our own weapons to escape destruction? They are watchful to annihilate us; shall we not be watchful to survive?

In the proper place we shall speak more particularly of these Christian weapons. In the meantime, to put it briefly, anyone who is going to fight those seven nations of the Canaanites, Kenizzites, Amorites, Perizites, Girgashites, Hivites, and Jebusites[1]—that is to say, when he has to fight the whole cohort of sins, of which the seven capital ones are considered the most deadly—this man should provide himself with two special weapons. That we should always be armed with prayer and with knowledge is the wish of Paul, who commands us to pray without ceasing.[2] Undefiled prayer lifts our spirits heavenward, a citadel manifestly inaccessible to the enemy. Knowledge puts the intellect in touch with salutary ideas. Neither, therefore, should be unsupported by the other:

> So each one claims
> The other's aid, and amiably combines with it.[3]

Prayer, indeed, makes intercession; but knowledge suggests what ought to be prayed for. Faith and hope make it possible for one to pray fervently and, as James puts it, without wavering;[4] knowledge shows one how to pray in the name of Jesus, that is, for things spiritually wholesome. The sons of Zebedee heard Christ say, "You don't know what you are asking."[5]

Prayer, of course, is the more potent, for it is communication with Deity; but knowledge is no less necessary. I am not at all sure that after you have fled from Egypt you should begin so long and hazardous a journey except under the leadership of both Moses and Aaron. The latter, having charge of the holy sacraments, serves as a symbol of prayer, whereas

Moses stands for knowledge of the law. But just as knowledge should not be crippled, so prayer should not be spiritless. Moses fought the enemy with the weapons of prayer, but with his hands held high. As soon as he let them fall, Israel had the worst of it.[6]

When you pray, do you by any chance consider only how many psalms you mumble your way through? Do you think the virtue of prayer lies in longwindedness? This is the great failing of those who, only infants as yet, have never outgrown the literal sense and ripened to spiritual maturity. Listen to what Christ teaches us in Matthew: "But when you pray, do not talk too much, as the heathen do; they think they will be heard for their verbosity. Do not be like them. Your Father knows what is good for you before you ask Him."[7] And Paul scorns ten thousand words of oral bombast, preferring five uttered in understanding.[8] Moses did not say a word; nevertheless, he heard the answer: "Why are you calling to me?"[9]

Not the outcry of the mouth but the burning desire of the spirit gets, like some very penetrating voice, a hearing from God. You should, then, make this your regular practice: as soon as the enemy falls upon you and vices you have abandoned tempt you, you should immediately lift your thoughts to heaven, from whence will come your help.[10] But be sure to lift your hands in that direction also. It is the safest course to be busy in righteous action, so that your efforts may be ascribed, not to earthly interests, but to Christ. But to avoid the mistake of despising the advantages of knowledge, consider this point: at one time it was enough for Israel to flee from the enemy; they were never so hardy as to provoke the Amalekites and fight it out with them hand to hand until they were fortified with manna from heaven and water pouring from the rock.[11] Strengthened by this nourishment, that notable warrior David scorned the whole host of the foe: "You have prepared a table in my sight against all who trouble us."[12]

Believe me, brother most dear to my heart, no onslaught of the adversary is so violent, no temptation is so strong, that the eager study of sacred letters cannot easily check them. No adversity is so painful that it cannot be made endurable. And, lest I seem a somewhat too unconventional expounder of scripture (as a matter of fact, I could cite imposing authorities on my side), what can more fittingly adumbrate the knowledge of God's secret law than does manna? In the first place, the fact that it came not from earth but rained down from heaven indicates a distinction between human and divine learning, for all the Holy Scriptures are divinely inspired and originate with God as the Author.[13] The fact that it was only a small thing[14] signifies the paltriness of language, the vast mysteries contained in words which are, so to speak, crude and inadequate. The fact that it was shining white signifies that, whereas every doctrine of man is tinged by some darkness of error, the teaching of Christ is wholly pure and clear and sound. The fact that it was somewhat hard and roughish signifies the hidden meaning concealed in the literal sense. If one busies himself with this surface content—with the husk, so to speak—what is more harsh and unpalatable? Only those who had tasted merely this shell of the manna said, "This is a hard saying; who can hear it?"[15] But dig out the spiritual meaning and nothing is sweeter, nothing more nourishing. Moreover, in the Hebrew tongue manna means "what is this?"[16] and this meaning neatly applies to the Holy Scripture, which has nothing irrelevant in it, not even a jot or a tittle, nothing unworthy of close study or of being pondered over, nothing incompatible with the question "what is this?"

And it is a common practice of the Holy Spirit to use water as a symbol of knowledge of God's law. You read of the waters of refreshment, on whose banks David exulted in being brought up.[17] You read of the waters that wisdom brings to the extremity of every passage.[18] You read of that mystical river into whose shallows Ezekiel could not cross over, once he had entered it.[19] You read of the wells Abraham dug which, filled with earth by the Philistines, were again restored by Isaac.[20] You read of the twelve wells where the drooping Israelites were revived after they had gone through the forty mansions.[21] In the Gospel you read of the well where Jesus sat while on a journey.[22] You read of the waters of Siloam, where He sent the blind man to recover his sight.[23] You read of the water poured into a basin to wash the feet of the Apostles.[24] And, not to explicate them all one by one, the frequent references in sacred writings to wells, fountains, and rivers suggest to us nothing less than a diligent scrutiny of the secret meanings of Scripture. For what is water hidden in the heart of the earth but mysterious truth hidden under the literal sense? And what is this same water bubbling up as a spring but that mystery opened up and illuminated? And when this is amplified in both length and breadth, why should it not be called a river?

Therefore, if you will devote yourself earnestly to the study of the Scripture, if you will ponder the law of the Lord both day and night, you will have no fear either by night or day, but be disciplined and trained against every onslaught of the adversary.[25] As a matter of fact, for the early stages of this campaigning I would not disapprove of the new recruit's getting some practice in the works of pagan poets and philosophers; only let him take them up in moderation, in a way appropriate to his immaturity and, so to speak, in passing—without expending his life on them and rotting, as it were, on the crags of the Sirens. To such studies as these Saint Basil calls the young men he educated in Christian character,[26] and our Augustine called his friend Licentius back to the Muses.[27] Nor does Jerome regret his loving a woman taken prisoner in war,[28] and Cyprian is praised because he enriched the temple of the Lord with the wealth of Egypt.[29]

I would by no means have you adopt the moral habits of

the pagans as a result of studying their literature, but you may find much in such sources that is otherwise conducive to right living. And whatever good advice even a pagan author gives ought not to be scorned, seeing that Moses did not spurn the counsel of his father-in-law, Jethro.[30] Literature shapes and invigorates the youthful character and prepares one marvelously well for understanding Holy Scripture, to pounce upon which with unscrubbed hands and feet is something akin to sacrilege. Jerome chides the effrontery of those who, coming straight out of secular studies, dare to expound the Scriptures;[31] but how much more impudent is the behavior of those people who presume to do that very same thing without even a taste of those disciplines!

However, just as divine Scripture bears no great fruit if you persist in clinging only to the literal sense, so the poetry of Homer and Vergil is of no small benefit if you remember that this is all allegorical, a fact which no one who has but touched his lips to the wisdom of the ancients will deny. I would advise you, though, not to handle the lewd poets at all, or at least not to study them too closely—unless you perhaps learn how to better avoid the vices described in their works and through the antithesis of immorality attain to love of virtue. I should prefer, too, that you follow the Platonists among the philosophers, because in most of their ideas and in their very manner of speaking they come nearest to the beauty of the prophets and the gospels.

In short, it will be profitable to study all pagan literature, provided you do it, as I have already said, at a suitable age and with discrimination—not only warily and judiciously, but also rapidly, like someone just traveling through rather than taking up residence there.

Finally—something especially important—let everything be related to Christ. To the pure all things are pure, whereas to the dirty, on the other hand, nothing is clean;[32] and it will be nothing against you if, like Solomon, you keep at home sixty queens, eighty concubines, and innumerable virgins[33] of the secular sciences, provided only that divine wisdom is, above all the rest, your dove, your thing of beauty, your best beloved. Ensnared by her beauty, an Israelite loves an alien woman, but after shaving her hair and cutting her nails, he makes an Israelite out of a foreigner.[34] Hosea marries a prostitute—indeed, he has children by her, not for himself but for the Lord of Sabbath—and the consecrated passion of the prophet increases the family of God.[35] After the Hebrews had left Egypt they lived for a while on unleavened bread, but this food was a stopgap and could not provision so great a journey.[36] Therefore, as soon as this palls upon you, you must turn to manna, or heavenly wisdom, as quickly as possible. It will nourish and invigorate you abundantly until you triumphantly capture those rewarding palms which never wither.

But in the meantime you must remember that one should not touch the Holy Scripture except with washed hands— this is to say, with absolute purity of mind—lest sin's antidote be turned into poison for you and the manna turn rancid.[37] Remember that unless you absorb it into the innermost recesses of mind and feeling, you will suffer the same fate as Uzzah, who had the temerity to lay profane hands upon the swaying ark and paid for his impermissible service with sudden death.[38] It is of prime importance to understand the value of these writings. Think of them as genuine oracles, as they are, originating in the secret depths of the mind of God. If you approach them reverently, with veneration and humility, you will perceive yourself to be possessed by His will, to be ineffably rapt and transported. You will experience the delights of His blessed Spirit, you will know the riches of Solomon, you will find the hidden storehouse of everlasting wisdom. But beware of brazenly forcing your way into the chambers. The door is low; see that you do not bump your head and bounce back!

Consider, too, that none of those things you see ?
eyes and touch with your hands are as real as the ?
read there, so that if heaven and earth were to pass away,
from God's Word not one jot or iota would pass away, but
that all will come to pass. Remember that men lie, that they
are deceived, but that the truth of God neither misleads nor
is itself misled.

From the interpretations of divine Scripture choose those
which go as far as possible beyond literal meaning. After
Paul, the best of the explicators of this sort are Origen, Ambrose, Jerome, and Augustine; for I see modern theologians
more willing to stick to the letter and to spend their energy
upon certain sophistical subtleties than upon the illumination of hidden meanings, as if Paul did not really say that
our law is of the spirit.[39]

I have heard several of these divines who were so smug
about their trivial little fictions that they scorned the exegeses
of earlier writers almost as they would the expounding of
dreams; Duns Scotus gave them such confidence that they
considered themselves master theologians without even
reading the sacred texts. But even if they do speak very
cleverly, let other men judge whether they have said anything worthy of the Holy Spirit. If you prefer to be sounder
in spirit than cunning in debate, if you are looking for food
for the soul rather than a show of ingenuity, then meditate
most profoundly upon the ancient commentators, whose
goodness is more reliably tested, whose learning is more
copious and mellow, whose language is neither dry nor
crude, and whose interpretations are more in keeping with
the spiritual content.[40]

I say this, not because I reject the moderns, but because I
prefer what is more useful and conducive to achieving your
purpose. Moreover, God's Spirit has its own language and
its own imagery, which you must, by all means, study carefully. When it speaks to us, this holy Wisdom stammers

childishly and, just like a solicitous mother, suits her speech to our own inadequacy.[41] She offers her milk to those who are little babes in Christ, Her herbs to those with weak stomachs. But naturally you should hasten to mature and get ready for more solid nourishment. She stoops to your incompetence; but you, conversely, should mount upward toward Her sublimity. To be always the infant is unnatural; to be always the invalid is too flabby. If you break through the husk and find the kernel, pondering one little line will have more savor and food value than will the whole psaltery when it is chanted through with reference only to the literal content, a fact which I stress the more earnestly as I know by experience that this error has captured the minds, not only of the common run of men, but even of those who in their vestments and titles make a profession of highly developed worship. As a result they think the ultimate in piety consists of just one thing: the daily repetition of as many psalms as they happen to know, although these are hardly understood, even literally.

Nor do I find any other reason for the fact that we see monastic devotion everywhere growing lax and enervated and dying out, but that these men are decaying in literalism and not striving for insight into the spiritual meaning of the Scriptures. They do not hear Christ calling out in the Gospels: "The flesh is good for nothing at all. It is the spirit that gives life."[42] They do not hear Paul corroborating his Master: "The letter kills; it is the spirit that quickens."[43] We know that since the law is of the spirit it is not of the flesh."[44] "Things of the spirit must be compared with things of the spirit."[45] At one time the Father of things spiritual wanted to be worshiped on a mountain top, but now in spirit.[46]

By no means, however, do I condemn the weakness of those who, constrained by their own intellectual limitations, do what they can by reciting the mystical psalms with simple and genuine faith. On the contrary, just as in superstitious incantations they pronounce certain words they do not understand, but which nevertheless are believed to work, so the sacred words, though but ill understood, one must suppose helpful to those who speak them or hear them with sincere trust and genuine feeling, and that attendant angels who *do* understand are summoned to bring them aid.

Nor does Paul, indeed, despise those people who sing psalms or speak with tongues; but he urges them to cultivate better spiritual gifts.[47] And if through some deficiency, not of inclination but of nature, a man cannot attain to this state, let him at least not rail at those who do seek greater spiritual power. As Paul puts it, the man who eats should not scorn the man who does not, and the one who does not should not judge the person who does.[48] Nevertheless, I should not want you, so well endowed with talent, to bog down in sterile literality, but to hurry on to more profound meanings and to bolster with frequent prayers the unflagging efforts of industry until the book closed with seven seals be opened to you. This it is which has the key of David, who also closes it; and no one reveals the secret mysteries of the Father, which only His Son knows, and whomever the Son has wished to unveil them to.[49]

But what a sidetrack is our discourse taking! My intention was to outline a way of life for you, not a course of study. As a matter of fact, we digressed to this extent while we were trying to show you a suitable workshop, where you should look for new weapons appropriate to your new warfare. To return to your instruction, then: if you will single out the best things from books of pagan authors and, after the manner of the bee, flying around over the gardens of antiquity, avoid the poison and suck out only the wholesome and profitable juice, you will to no small extent make your character better equipped for that kind of satisfactory living with others which the ancients call "ethical." Certainly, a number of the weapons in the armory of their wisdom should by no means be despised.

Consider, moreover, that any truth you come upon at any place is Christ's. That divine shield of Vulcan[50] (as the poets put it), impervious to every weapon, is drawn from nothing but the arsenal of Holy Scripture, where our commander David has amassed for his soldiery the whole machinery of war, by means of which they may battle the uncircumcised Philistines either at long range or close quarters.[51] With these arms Homer's Achilles was not protected, nor Vergil's Aeneas, even if they are so represented. One of them was shamefully overcome by anger and the other by passion.

Nor is it a foolish saying that these arms are forged, not in the workshops of men, but in those Vulcan shared with Minerva. For poets who depict the gods assign to Minerva the province of arts and sciences, and to Vulcan that of fire. I think this is what actually happens when the fire of divine love finally tempers a character refined by noble learning:

> Even if the universe should tumble in ruins,
> It would strike a man undaunted.[52]

But first you must get rid of the arms of arrogant Saul, which are more burdensome than useful and which hindered David more than they helped him when he was about to meet Goliath.[53] Next, from the bank of the stream of mystical Scriptures you should gather five pebbles, signifying, perhaps, the five words Paul uses "in understanding."[54] Finally, take the sling in your right hand. With these arms that one and only enemy of ours, Satan, the father of pride, is at last laid low. How did our Captain, Jesus Christ, finally overcome him completely? Did he not reply to the tempter with words of Holy Scripture, just as if He were striking the forehead of the foe with pebbles gathered from the stream?[55]

And would you like to hear about the arms of the Christian Pallas? "He will take up His zeal as armor," says the Scripture, "and equip His creature for vengeance upon the enemy. He will put on justice as a breastplate and receive sound judgment as a helmet; he will take up the impenetrable shield of equity and sharpen stern anger into a spear."[56] In Isaiah you read this: "He was harnessed in righteousness as in a cuirass and the helmet of salvation was on his head. He was clad in the garments of vengeance and covered, as it were, by the cloak of zeal."[59]

And if you wish to go now to the armory of Paul, a chieftain by no means sluggish, you will find unequivocally that the weapons of our warfare are not material ones, but that, in God, they are mighty in leveling fortifications, foiling stratagems, and reducing every tower erected against the wisdom of God.[58] You will find there the Lord's harness, with which you can resist in the day of evil. You will find the weapons of justice on the right hand and on the left; you will find truth, the cover for your body, the breastplate of justice and the shield of faith, upon which you can extinguish all the fiery missiles of malignant Satan. You will find the helmet of righteousness and the sword of the spirit, which is the Word of God.[59]

Anyone carefully shielded and protected by all of these will at last be able to speak out boldly those dauntless words of Paul: "Who, then, shall separate us from the love of Christ? Shall hardship or poverty or hunger or nakedness or peril or persecution or the sword? See what a mighty adversary, so fearsome to all men, He reduces to nothing."

But listen to something even stronger, for he goes on: "But in all these things we are triumphant because of Him who loved us. For I am assured that neither death nor life, neither angels nor principalities, nor virtues, nor things present, nor things to come, nor strength, nor height, nor depth, nor any other thing in creation will be able to separate us from the love of God, which is in Christ Jesus."[60]

What joyful confidence the weapons of light give Paul—

that is, to a little man who calls himself a despicable outcast of this world![61] Such strength of arms, therefore, the Holy Scriptures will provide for you if you turn to them wholeheartedly, that you will need no counsel of ours. But since you so wish it, let me not seem unaccommodating.

I have fashioned for you an *enchiridion*, that is to say, a kind of hand dagger, which you should never put aside, not even at the table or in bed, so that even if you must sojourn at times in the business of this world and find it cumbersome to carry around that whole armor, nevertheless you will not expose yourself at any time and have the waylayer pounce upon you completely unprepared. At least it should not be inconvenient to keep with you this little blade, which will never be very heavy or ineffectual in guarding yourself. It is quite small, but understand that if you use it in conjunction with a little shield of faith you will easily sustain the tumultuous assault of the enemy without suffering any deadly wound.

But now it is time for us to try to pass on some methods of wielding the weapons, which, if you diligently practice, I am confident that Christ, our Leader, will bring you off the winner out of this garrison and into His state of Jerusalem in triumph, where there is no clamor of war at all, but deathless peace and perfect tranquillity. In the meantime, however, all hope of salvation lies in this steel.

FOUR

The First Point of Wisdom Is to Know Yourself; Concerning Two Kinds of Wisdom: Seeming and Real

PEACE IS THAT ultimate good toward which even the lovers of this world bend all their efforts, but, as I have already said, they grasp at a counterfeit kind. Philosophers used falsely to promise peace to the followers of their teachings, but only Christ bestows that which the world is not able to give.[1] There is only one way of arriving at this peace: to make war upon ourselves, to battle fiercely against our own vices. Toward these foes God, who is our peace, is implacably hostile because His nature is virtue itself, as well as the parent and author of all virtue.

Now, the general mixture of all kinds of vice is called *stultitia*, or folly, by the Stoics, those very stout defenders of virtue; in our Scripture it is called *malicia*, or wickedness. Similarly, complete probity in every respect is, in both quarters, called *sapientia*—wisdom. Does not wisdom, moreover—by Wisdom's own declaration[2]—overcome wickedness? Belial, the ruler of wickedness, is the father and prince of darkness; whoever follows his leadership is walking in night and hurrying toward an everlasting night. On the other hand, the author of wisdom—rather, Wisdom itself—is Christ Jesus, who is the true light, the only light dispelling the night of worldly folly; the radiance of His Father's glory who, according to Paul, was made our wisdom when He became the redemption and justification for us who have been reborn in Him.[3]

"We preach Christ crucified," he says, "to the Jews a stumbling block and to the Gentiles foolishness; but to those who

have been called, both Jews and Gentiles, we preach Christ
as God's excellence and God's wisdom,"[4] through which, and
following His example, we can overcome our enemy, wickedness, if only we are wise in Him, in whom we shall conquer.

This is what you must cling to, rejecting the wisdom of
the world, which tries to sell itself to fools under the most
deceiving labels. For, as Paul says, in the eyes of God there
is no more profound folly than worldly wisdom: it must be
unlearned by one who wishes to be truly wise. "If anyone
among you," he continues, "seems wise in this world, let him
become a fool in order that he may be wise, for the wisdom
of this world is folly with God."[5] And a little before this he
says, "For it is written that I shall cast away the wisdom of
the wise and reject the understanding of the prudent. Where
is the wise man? Where is the scribe? Where is he who pries
into temporal knowledge? Has God not made foolish the wisdom of this world?"[6]

I have no doubt that already these clever fools are hatefully
yammering at you and, blind leaders of blind followers,[7] crying out that you are crazy, raving, lunatic, because you are
preparing to go over to Christ. These fellows are Christians
only in name; more accurately, they are both mockers and
assailants of Christ's teachings. Do not let yourself be affected by any of the babbling of those people whose blindness is to be pitied and deplored, not adopted.

For what is it but a perverted sort of shrewdness to be
expert and deft in matters trifling and nugatory, even shameful, but to have no more understanding than a beast of those
things which alone pertain to our spiritual health? Paul
would have us be wise in goodness, simple concerning evil.[8]
Those others are clever in the performance of iniquity but
know nothing about doing good. And when that eloquent
Greek poet Hesiod considers a man good for nothing if,
knowing nothing himself, he pays no attention to good
advice others give him,[9] what shall we think of those who,

themselves execrably deluded, never leave off mocking, heckling, and intimidating people who have already come to their senses? Will not the mocker be mocked? He that lives in heaven will laugh at them in turn; the Lord will jeer at them.[10] In the Book of Wisdom you read that they will see Him and reject Him, but that God will laugh them to scorn.[11]

To be laughed at by evil men is, in effect, to be praised; surely it is a wonderful thing to vie with the Apostles and with Christ, our Head. But by the same token it is a fearful thing to be mocked by God. "I too will laugh at your destruction," says Wisdom, "and I will jeer at you when that thing you feared comes to pass"; which is to say, when those people who have waked up too late will cry, "These are the people we once held objects of scorn and ridicule. Stupidly we considered their life madness and their end without honor."[12]

That, as James says, is a brutish, a devilish wisdom, alien to God.[13] Its end is death, and attending it always is its pernicious handmaiden, presumption, with blindness of heart following presumption, tyranny of passions following blindness, plus the license to sin as much as you like. After that license comes habit, and following habit the most luckless insensibility of mind, whereby is lost all awareness of evil. Then physical death overtakes men in this insensible condition, and a second death follows the physical. So you see that the wisdom of worldliness is mother to the greatest mischief.

Concerning the wisdom of Christ, however, which the world considers foolishness, you read this: "With her all good things have come to me at once, and countless honors from her hands. And I rejoiced in them all because that wisdom went before me, and I did not know that she is the mother of all good things."[14] She brings as her attendants modesty and gentleness. Gentleness makes us receptive to the Holy Spirit, for it rejoices to hover over the humble and mild.[15] And when it has steeped our minds in its sevenfold anointment, then at length flourishes that rich harvest of all virtue and its blessed fruits, the best of which is that inward and secret joy known only by those who have achieved it, a joy which does not vanish and melt away with the delights of this world, but expands and swells into bliss everlasting. This wisdom, my brother, we ought to seek from God, as James counsels us,[16] with our most fervent prayers and, in the words of a certain wise man, mine this hidden treasure out of the veins of Holy Scripture.[17]

The chief point of this wisdom is simply to know yourself, an injunction which antiquity believed to have originated in heaven and which great authors have found so pleasing that they consider the whole fruit of wisdom compactly enclosed in it.[18] The aphorism should carry little weight with us, however, unless it agrees with our own literature. Now, that mystical lover in the Canticles threatens his bride and orders her to get out of the house unless she understand herself: "If you do not know yourself, O beautiful among women, go forth and walk in the footsteps of the flocks."[19]

Even so, no man should rashly pride himself on understanding everything there is to know about himself. I doubt that anyone completely understands even his own body; how, then, can he be fully acquainted with the nature of his mind? Although Paul had been allowed to penetrate the mysteries of the third heaven,[20] he did not dare judge himself, as he surely would have dared had he known himself well enough. Now, if a man so spiritual and discerning in every respect—one not to be judged by anyone else—if even he understood himself imperfectly, how can we carnal men be so confident?

Of course, a man who does not consider that he knows all there is to know about his own forces or those of the enemy may seem a very inept soldier, but this war is not between man and man, but between man and himself. Indeed, the battle array of the foe emerges from the depths of our own nature, just like the earth-born brothers of poetic fiction.[21] Moreover, there is so little difference between friend and enemy that we are in grave danger of unwarily defending enemy as friend, or hurting friend in place of enemy. One notable captain was not even sure about an angel of light: "Are you one of us," he asked, "or of the foe?"[22]

Since you have declared war upon yourself, therefore, and in this contest the chief hope of victory lies in your knowing yourself as thoroughly as possible, I shall set up a kind of image for you—on a tablet, so to speak—so that you may clearly understand what you are like inwardly, what you are, under the skin.

FIVE

Concerning the Inner and Outer Man

MAN, THEN, IS a being of a most unusual sort, composed of two or three vastly unlike parts: a soul that is like something divine and a body like that of a dumb brute. In physical terms, obviously, we do not excel every other animal in every respect, but in each of their special gifts are found to be inferior. In regard to soul, however, we have that capacity for the divine which enables us to surpass even the nature of angels and be made one with God. If you had not been given a body, you would be part of Godhead; if you had not been endowed with this mind of yours, you would be a beast.[1]

These two natures, so dissimilar to each other, the Supreme Artist once had united in felicitous harmony; but the serpent, enemy of peace, alienated them with jarring discord, so that now they can neither be separated without the utmost torment nor live together without continuous warfare. Obviously, as the saying has it, each in the other is holding a wolf

;[2] and a very clever bit of verse applies equally
:

_ can live neither with you nor without you.[3]

As a result we are inwardly torn by an involved kind of
dissension as elements are simultaneously one with and at
odds with each other. Because the body is itself visible, it
takes pleasure in visible objects; because it is mortal, it pursues temporal objects; because it has weight and substance,
its tendency is downward. The soul, on the other hand, mindful of its celestial quality, yearns mightily to ascend, and
struggles against its earthly encumbrance; it spurns those
things which are visible for it knows they are ephemeral; it
seeks those things which are true and eternal. Being immortal
it is in love with immortal objects; being celestial it cherishes
the celestial. Like is attracted to like, provided the soul has
not been utterly besotted by the body's foulness and, as a
result of that contamination, degenerated from its original
fineness.

Nor was it fabled Prometheus[4] who planted this disso-
nance in us, mixing in with our mind a little bit of every
beast; nor did our original state furnish it. Rather, sin has
evilly corrupted what was happily created, injecting the
venom of discord into things once well attuned. For at one
time the mind ruled the body without difficulty, and the
body willingly and gladly obeyed; now, quite to the contrary, the rightful order of things having been disrupted,
physical passions try to dictate to reason and reason is com-
pelled to give way before the desires of the body. As a result,
one may appropriately liken the breast of man to a sort of
factious commonwealth which, consisting of varying classes
of men with clashing interests, is bound to be shaken by
frequent disturbances and commotions unless one man has
the supremacy of power, and unless that man has such char-

acter that he imposes only what is conducive to the well-being of the state.

For that reason it is necessary that the wise should command and the less competent should obey. Now, there is nothing more senseless than the mob; they should, therefore, be ruled by magistrates and have no offices themselves. Those who are better qualified or riper in years ought, of course, to be listened to in an advisory capacity; but only so long as the power of decision remains in the hands of one ruler, who may very well be counseled from time to time, but not coerced or overruled. This king, in turn, is subject only to the law; and law is a reflection of the absolute idea of Right.

But if, in a senseless reversal of order, the unbridled masses, the tumultuous dregs of the state, struggle to supersede their superiors, or if the lords disregard the authority of the king, perilous discord springs up in our state and—barring a rescue by God's intercession—the whole commonwealth heads toward utter chaos.

Now, reason in man serves as king. Certain of the feelings —physical, it is true, but not so bestial as others—you may consider as nobles. These higher emotions include the natural respect for parents, love for brothers, kindliness toward friends, pity for the afflicted, fear of dishonor, eagerness for honorable reputation, and the like. But those perturbations of passions which jar strongly against the principles of reason and grovel abjectly at brute level—these you should consider equivalent to the very dregs of the mob. Of this sort are lust, debauchery, envy, and comparable sicknesses of the mind which, like faithless and degenerate slaves, must without exception be held in check so that they can, if possible, perform their prescribed work for their master, and if not, at least do no real harm.

All of this a divinely wise Plato has written of in the

Timaeus,[5] how the sons of the gods had made man in their
own likeness and provided him with two kinds of soul. One
part was godlike and immortal; the other, not far from mortal,
and subject to various disorders, first of which was voluptuousness—the bait of evil, as he puts it. Next was grief, an
avoidance of and impediment to good; after that, fear and
rashness, mad counselors attended by implacable wrath.
Then came seductive hope, along with senseless emotional-
ism and amorous desire, the usurper of everything else.

These are the virtual words of Plato. Nor was he unaware
that the happy life lay in controlling upheavals of this sort,
for in this same work he writes that those who have triumphed
over such passions will live rightly, but those mastered by
them will live badly. And he fixed the seat of the immortal
soul—that is, reason—in the brain, like the residence of a
king in the citadel of our state, the loftiest part of the body,
obviously, the one closest to heaven and the least brutish,
seeing that it has a thin bone and is clogged neither by
sinews nor flesh, but strongly fortified within and without
by powers of perception so that no turmoil could spring up
in the state which reason, informed by those powers, should
not at once know about.

But the parts of the mortal soul, which is to say the passions, he separated from reason at a distance corresponding
to their compliance or disagreement with it. Between neck
and diaphragm he placed that part of the soul having to do
with manly courage and wrathfulness, emotions certainly
factious and to be kept in check; but since this is a part not
so brutish he set it midway between the highest and lowest
conditions lest, in too close vicinity to either, it might trouble
the calm of the ruler or, infected by the taint of the basest
passions, conspire with them against reason.

Last of all, sensual appetite, which lusts for the pleasure
of food and drink and which drives us into erotic love, he
relegated to liver and bowels—below the midriff and far

from reason's stronghold—like some kind of untamed and intractable beast; there it should be penned, since it was in the habit of causing the most violent upheavals and was not at all amenable to rational control. Just how beastly and intractable this lowest part of our nature is, the pudenda of the body can demonstrate, in which area it exercises the most absolute tyranny. With its foul incitements it, alone of all the members, continually promotes rebellion in spite of the king's fruitless protests.

So, in this you surely see that man, a godlike creature above, tails off into brutishness. But that divine counselor presiding in the lofty citadel, mindful of his origin, purposes nothing sordid or base. His mark of distinction is an ivory sceptre, because he never misgoverns; and Homer writes that on his head an eagle sits:[6] soaring up toward the heavens, reason looks down with piercing eyes upon things of earth. Finally, he wears a golden crown. In mystical literature gold commonly signifies wisdom. The circular shape of the crown, moreover, symbolizes perfection and completeness in every respect.

These are the gifts appropriate to kings: first, that they have as much wisdom as possible in order to avoid committing a wrong through error; next, that whatever is right, this only they wish for, so that they may do nothing falsely or meanly or contrary to reason. Anyone lacking in one of these qualities you should consider, not a ruler, but a thief.

SIX

Concerning the Variety of Passions

THIS KING OF ours, it is true, is vulnerable to assault; but, through an eternal law of God imposed upon him, he cannot be so corrupted that he does not protest or resist. If the rest of the subjects will but obey him, he will do nothing ever to be regretted, nothing dishonorable, but will conduct every affair with the utmost moderation and composure.

Stoics and Peripatetics differ about the passions in several respects, of course, although they all agree that we ought to live according to reason rather thán feeling. The Stoics will have it that when you have used the passions, which are especially susceptible to sensual stimulation, as preceptors and have arrived at a valid judgment and ability to discriminate between what you should court and what avoid, then you should shun them altogether; for then they are not only useless in the cultivation of wisdom, but downright harmful. For this reason they want their perfect wise man to be free of all perturbations of this sort, as if these were sicknesses of the mind; and some of the more exacting will scarely allow a wise man even those first extra-rational impulses which they call *phantasiae*, or fancies.

The Peripatetics, however, teach that the passions are not to be extirpated but controlled, for they are of the opinion that some of them are useful because they have been implanted by nature as a kind of incentive and spur to virtue, as anger contributes to courage, envy to industry, and so on. But in Plato's *Phaedo* Socrates seems indisputably on the side of the Stoics, since he holds that philosophy is nothing but a practicing of death—which is to say that the mind, insofar as it can, withdraws from the physical and sensible world and applies itself to those things perceptible only to reason, not to sense.[1]

The first thing you must do, therefore, is to understand all these agitations of the mind; then you must realize that there are none so turbulent that they cannot be curbed by rational control or channeled in the direction of virtue. Everywhere I hear people expressing the noxious belief that they are driven into vice. And, on the other hand, some persons who know nothing of themselves follow passions of this sort camouflaged as the dictates of reason, as when they call "godly zeal" that which was really inspired by anger or envy. And just as one commonwealth is more discordant than another, so one man is more inclined to virtue than another, a difference which proceeds not from inequality of mental powers, but either from the influence of celestial bodies or from his ancestors or his youthful upbringing or his very physical condition.

Socrates' fable of the charioteers and their horses, good and bad, is not inapropos.[2] For you see some born with a temperate character, so tractable and amenable that they may be trained in virtue without difficulty and outstrip the rest without spurring. On the other hand, some have a rebellious body, an unbroken and refractory horse, so to speak; and the result is that even with the harshest bit, spurs, and club, the sweating driver has trouble taming its wildness.

Now if by chance such is your lot, do not lose heart forthwith, but struggle that much harder. Look at it this way: the path to virtue has not been barred to you; instead, you have been presented with more abundant material for virtue. And if you have been endowed with a good character, you are not straightway better than another person for this reason, but luckier; and not only that, but the more fortunate you are, the more you are bound by obligations. For that matter, who is so felicitously equipped by nature that he does not find a great many things he has to resist?

Wherever he finds himself especially open to rebellion, then, in this quarter the ruler must be particularly vigilant. Certain vices are virtually indigenous, just as they say treachery is common in some countries, debauchery in others, lechery in still others. Some vices depend on the condition of the body: for example, a fondness for women and love of pleasure are characteristic of sanguine men; wrath, fierceness, and foul speech, of the choleric; sluggishness and idleness, of the phlegmatic; envy, gloom, bitterness, of the melancholic.[3] Some vices either slacken or flourish according to a man's age: in youth, for instance, come lust, extravagance, and recklessness; in old age, stinginess, moroseness, and greed. And some seem peculiar to a particular sex: fierceness to the male, vanity and vengefulness to the female.

It sometimes happens that nature, as if equalizing matters, compensates for a frailty in character with some contrasting gift. One man has a propensity for sensual pleasure but is not at all wrathful or envious. Another is chaste, but somewhat lofty, somewhat hot-tempered, somewhat tightfisted. Nor is there any lack of those who are harassed by certain ruinous and monstrous vices; thieving, sacrilege, murder, which indeed have to be shunned with all one's might and the brazen wall[4] of strict principles thrown up against their assault.

On the other hand, several passions so closely resemble virtues that we risk being misled into confusing one with the other. These failings must be corrected and appropriately turned in the direction of the virtue they resemble. For example, if someone of rather inflammable temper will apply the curb to his spirit, he will be rather brisk, full of vitality, not so dull. He will be frank and direct. Or suppose another person is a bit niggardly: let him apply reason here, and he will be frugal. If one is inclined to be obsequious, let him become merely friendly and agreeable; if he is stubborn, let him become steadfast; if he is rather gloomy, let him become sober; if he is prone to foolery, let him become merely congenial. And so on with the rest of these lesser defects of character.

In this connection let us be careful not to dress up a vice of nature with the name of virtue, calling moroseness gravity, harshness justice, envy zeal, stinginess thrift, fawning friendliness, scurrility good fellowship.

This, therefore, is the only way to virtue: first, that you know yourself; second, that you act, not according to the passions, but the dictates of reason. And let reason be sound and healthful; that is, let it look only to what is honorable.

"But," you will say, "what you prescribe is difficult!"

Who says it is not? There is truth, though, in Plato's remark that whatever is excellent is also hard.[5] Nothing is harder than conquering oneself, but no reward is greater than felicity. Jerome puts it admirably, as he does everything: "No one is happier than the Christian, for he has the assurance of the Kingdom of Heaven. No one is more troubled than he, for he daily puts his life in jeopardy. No one is stronger than he, for he overcomes the Devil. No one is weaker than he, for he is overcome by the flesh."[6] If you weigh only your own resources, nothing is harder than to subject the flesh to the spirit; but if you look upon God as your helper, nothing is easier. Only seize with a stout heart upon the principle of the perfect life and press forward in your purpose. Never yet has the human spirit failed to accomplish something it ardently demanded of itself. A large part of the Christian life is to wish wholeheartedly to become a Christian; what will seem unattainable at the outset will become more accessible as you approach it, easy when you use it, and, at last, delightful when you get accustomed to it.

Hesiod has a well-known saying:

Hard, at first, is the way of virtue,
But after you have painfully crawled to the summit
The surest peace awaits you.[7]

No beast is so fierce that it cannot be gentled by human effort; will there be no way of gentling the character of him who tames everything else? To be physically strong, you can for some years make yourself temperate in drinking and in sexual intercourse, restraints your human physician has prescribed. In order to spend life tranquilly, then, can you not control your passions a few short months, something God, your Creator, commands? To ward off bodily illness you do everything possible; to save body and soul from eternal death, are you not going to do the things which even pagans have done?

SEVEN

Concerning the Inner and Outer Man and the Two Aspects of Man according to Holy Scripture

TRULY, I AM ashamed for Christian men, most of whom like dumb brutes are enslaved to their appetites and have been so little disciplined in this warfare that they do not even know the difference between reason and passion. They think that the man is only what they see and feel; in fact, they suppose that nothing exists except what is perceptible to the senses, though actually nothing is less true. Whatever they especially enjoy, that they think is right. Certain and lamentable bondage they call peace, while submissive reason, resisting nothing, follows wherever passion calls.

This is that wretched peace which Christ, who is the author of real peace and who made truth and peace one, came to dissolve, intending to stir up a saving warfare betweeen father and son, between husband and wife, between those things which a dishonorable harmony has evilly reconciled.[1] Now then, let the philosophers carry little weight, except for the fact that all these things are taught in the Holy Scriptures, though not in the same terms. What the philosophers call reason Paul sometimes refers to as spirit, sometimes as the inner man, sometimes as the law of mind. What they call passions he now calls the flesh, now the body, now the outward man, now the law of bodily members.

"Walk in the spirit," he says, "and you will not bring about the desires of the flesh; for the flesh covets things contrary to the spirit, and the spirit things contrary to the flesh, so that you may not do whatever you wish."[2] And elsewhere:

"Therefore, if you will live according to the flesh, you will die. If in the spirit you will have mortified the deeds of the flesh, you will live."[3] A new alteration of matters, certainly, that peace should be sought in war, war in peace, life in death, death in life, freedom in slavery, slavery in freedom. For in another place Paul writes: "I chastise my body and bring it under subjection."[4]

And hear about freedom: "Therefore, if you are led by the spirit you are not subject to the law."[5] And, "We have not received again the spirit of bondage in fear, but the spirit of adoption as sons of God."[6] And still again: "I see another law for my physical members, one resisting the law of my mind and enslaving me in the law of sin, which is in my members."[7] And you read in the same author about the outward man, which is corrupted, and the inner man, which is renewed from day to day.[8]

Plato puts two souls in one man; Paul, two men in the same man, so conjoined that neither may be divided from the other either in heaven or hell, but also so disparate that the death of one is the life of the other. This is the point, I think, of what he wrote to the Corinthians: "The first man was created a living soul; the last Adam, a life-giving spirit. The spiritual part was not first, however, but the physical. Then came that which is spirit. The first man was of the earth, earthly; the second, of heaven, celestial." And that these words might be more clearly applicable not only to Christ and Adam but to all of us, he appended this: "As one was of the earth, so are we; as one was of heaven, so are we. Therefore, if we have borne a likeness to the earthly, let us also bear a likeness to the celestial. But I say this, brothers: since flesh and blood will not possess the kingdom of God, neither will corruption possess the incorruptible."[9]

Do you not plainly see that what he elsewhere referred to as the flesh and as the outward man, which is corruptible, he calls the earthly Adam? This, surely, is that body of death oppressed by which Paul cried, "Oh, unhappy man that I am, who will free me from this body of death?"[10] Finally, explaining the widely diverse fruits of the flesh and the spirit, he writes again: "Whoever sows in his flesh will reap corruption from the flesh; whoever sows in the spirit will reap eternal life from the spirit."[11]

This, then, is that ancient disagreement between the twins Jacob and Esau, who before they were born were at odds with each other, even within the confines of the maternal womb. Esau, it is true, was born first, but Jacob carried off the blessing: first, that is to say, comes that which is carnal; but the spiritual part is more important. The one was red and hairy, the other beardless. One was restless, a hunter; the other delighted in domestic quiet. And because he was hungry, Esau sold the right due to the first born; seduced by the promise of paltry pleasure he abandoned the liberty he was born to for the bondage of sin. The other, by the trick of a favorite, got for himself what he was not entitled to by law.[12]

Between these brothers complete harmony was never established, even though they were carried in the same womb at the same time. For Esau hates Jacob, and Jacob, though he does not return hatred for hatred, nevertheless shuns Esau and always regards him with suspicion and distrust. Similarly, you should look with suspicion upon whatever passion persuades you to do, because of the dubious reliability of the advocate.

Jacob alone saw the Lord; Esau, as a bloodthirsty man, lived by the sword. In conclusion, when consulted by their mother, the Lord answered, "The elder shall be servant to the younger" and the father added, "You, Esau, will serve your brother. And the time will come when you will discard and shake off his yoke from your neck."[13]

Now the Lord here is prophesying about good men, the father about bad ones. One indicates what should be done by everyone; the other predicts what most men in fact are going to do.

Paul would have woman subordinate to the husband.[14] "The iniquity of the man is preferable to the goodness of the woman."[15] Our Eve is fleshly passion, whose eyes were daily lured by that crafty serpent; and when she had been corrupted, she hurried to entice man into sharing evil with her. But what do you read about the new woman, she, that is, who is obedient to her husband? "I will put enmity between you"—referring, of course, to the serpent and the woman— "and between your seed and hers. She will bruise your head, and you will lie in wait for her heel."[16] The serpent has been reduced to crawling on his belly; Christ's death has broken the fury of his attack: he now only furtively ambushes her heel. However, having been made manlike by the grace of faith, woman undauntedly grinds under her foot the venomous head. Her favor has been increased and the tyranny of the flesh has been diminished.

When Sarah's vigor lessened, Abraham, by the will of God, became greater and she then called him "lord" instead of "husband." Furthermore, she was not allowed to have a child until she had lost her womanly fertility. And when she was an old woman past the age for having children, what did she bear her lord, Abraham? Isaac, to be sure, or *joy*. Thus at the same time that the passions decline in man, then is born that happy tranquillity of an upright heart, that peace of mind which resembles the enjoyment of a perennial feast.

And just as Abraham did not grant liberties to his wife, so he looked distrustfully upon the playing together of the children, Isaac and Ishmael. Sarah did not want the son of a maid-servant to associate with the son of a free woman at that age, but demanded that Ishmael be banished from sight during his youth lest, by a show of congeniality, he attract the boy Isaac to his own habits. By this time Abraham was an old man and Sarah an old woman, and she had given birth to Isaac; but still the husband was not sure of the wife's counsel until God's pronouncement set the seal of approval upon it. He does not feel sure about the woman until he hears God say, "Listen to the words of Sarah in everything she has said."[17]

What a happy old age they have in whom that carnal man is thus quickly disposed of, so that it presents no problem to the spirit. Whether this perfect concord at all points may be achieved in this life I should not care to say. Perhaps it would not even be a good thing, for Paul was given the goad of the flesh, a messenger from Satan, to trouble him; and when he had asked the Lord for the third time to remove this goad, he heard only this reply: "Paul, my grace is enough for you, for virtue is achieved through weakness."[18] A new kind of remedy, surely! That Paul may not be proud, he is tempted by pride; that he may be strong in Christ, he is forced to be weak in himself. He was carrying the treasure of divine revelation in an earthen vessel so that the glory would attend, not himself, but the might of God.[19]

This one example of the Apostle instructs us equally well in a number of things. For one, when we are enticed by wickedness, we should pray repeatedly for God's help. For another, to devout men temptations are sometimes not hazardous, but even fruitful in the maintenance of virtue. And, finally, we are taught that when all the rest of the passions have been subjugated, only the infirmity of empty glory lies in ambush, even in the midst of virtues; and this is like that Hydra of Hercules, a monster tenacious of life and spawning by means of its own wounds; one which, even at the very end, when all other labors have been finished, can scarcely be suppressed. But persistent labor overcomes all difficulties.[20] In the meantime, when the mind seethes with furious upheavals you must, with every resource at your command, stick with and bind fast that Proteus of yours with tough chains, even as

into marvelous shapes he changes himself
Into fire and ravening beast and flowing river.[21]

And what, pray, is so Protean as the emotions and desires of fools when these draw their victims now into bestial lust, now into ferocious anger, now into poisonous envy, now into more and more monstrous forms of vice. Is this not a neatly appropriate bit which the most accomplished of all poets has written?

Then varying shapes will mock you, and the likenesses
    of beasts;
For suddenly he will become a bristly swine, a malev-
    olent tiger,
A scaly dragon, a tawny-throated lioness.
Or he will make the crackling sound of flames.[22]

But remember what follows:

Nevertheless, my son, the more shapes he assumes
The more tightly you must draw his stout bonds.[23]

Not that we need to keep returning to the stories of poets: follow the example of the holy patriarch Jacob in stead-fastly pressing the struggle throughout the night, until the dawn of God's help begins to shine. Say, "I shall not release you until you give me a blessing."[24]

And what that indomitable wrestler won as the prize for his strength is worth hearing about: first, God gave him a blessing on the spot, for always, after temptations have been overcome, a certain extraordinary increase of divine grace is added to a man, by means of which he is much more strongly fortified than before against the assault of the adversary. Second, after a touch on the thigh the sinew of the victor withered and he began to limp on the one foot. In the words of the prophet, God curses those who limp on both feet,[25] that is, those who want at the same time to please God and to live in a carnal manner, and while they are trying to do both, limp in both. But happy are those in whom carnal passion has died at God's touch, so that they lean most strongly upon the right foot, in other words, that of the spirit. As a final reward, his name was changed: instead of Jacob he became *Israel*, from the wrestler to the tranquil man.[26] When you have castigated your flesh and crucified it, along with its vices and desires,[27] then peace and repose will come to you without resistance so that you may be free to see the Lord, to see and enjoy Him, since the Lord is sweet. This is what *Israel* means.

Moreover, God is not seen in the fire or the whirlwind or the tumult of temptations. But following the Devil's hurricane there comes—if only you persevere—the gentle rustling of the breeze of spiritual comfort.[28] Once this has softly breathed upon you, listen closely with the inward ear and you will be Israel and will say with him, "I have seen the Lord, and my soul has been made whole."[29] You will see Him who has said, "No flesh will see me."[30]

Examine yourself. If you are flesh you will not see the Master. If you do not see Him, your soul will not be made whole. See to it, then, that you are spirit.

EIGHT

Concerning the Three Parts of Man: Spirit, Soul, and Flesh

THESE THINGS I have already written were considerably more than sufficient, but in order that you may become even a bit more perceptive about yourself, and more searching, it is advisable to consider briefly Origen's way of partitioning man. Like Paul he describes three parts: spirit, soul, and flesh.[1] Writing to the Thessalonians, the Apostle united all

of these so that, he says, "your body, soul, and spirit m.
kept blameless on the day of our Lord Jesus Christ."[2] Isa
however, mentions two, leaving out the lowest part: "N
soul," he says, "will long for you in the night, but in the morn-
ing I will watch for you in my spirit, in my heart."[3] Daniel
also says, "Let the spirits and souls of good men praise the
Lord."[4]

From these sources Origen not unreasonably deduces the
tripartite division of man: the body, or flesh, the basest part
of us upon which that crafty old serpent has foisted the law
of sin through our inborn taint, and by which we are incited
to shamefulness and made one with Satan if we yield; the
spirit, in which we assuredly express our resemblance to the
nature of God, upon which the supreme Artist inscribed
with his finger that eternal law of righteousness from the
archetype of his own Mind, that is, according to his own
Spirit. By this part we are cemented to God and made one
with Him. Finally, as the third part midway between these
two, He provided the soul, which has a share in our consciousness and perception as well as in our natural affections.

Just as a person in a strife-torn nation, the soul has to align
herself with one of the other parts. She is drawn this way and
that, but she is free to incline toward whichever part she
wishes. If, renouncing the flesh, she draws over to the
spiritual part, she will herself become spiritual; but if she
lowers herself to the desires of the flesh, she will herself
degenerate into carnality.

This is what Paul meant when he was writing to the
Corinthians: "But do you not know that when a man couples
with a harlot he is made one body with her? He who clings to
the Lord, however, is made one with the Spirit."[5] It is this
seductive part of man he calls a harlot. This element is that
alluring and provocative woman you read about in the second
chapter of Proverbs: "That you may escape the foreign
woman, one from another country, who makes soft her words

and abandons the husband of her youth and has forgot her
agreement with God. For her house is headed for death and
her ways toward hell. None who go to her will return, nor
will they find the path of life."[6] And in chapter six: "That
they may guard you from an evil woman and the seductive
tongue of a foreign woman, let your heart not desire her
beauty, let yourself not be trapped by her pleasures. For
the price of a harlot is scarcely a loaf of bread, but the woman
ravishes the precious soul of man."[7]

Now, when he mentioned the prostitute, the heart, and the
soul, did he not signify, one by one, the three divisions of
man?

Again, in chapter nine: "A foolish and noisy woman, full
of enticements and knowing nothing at all, sits upon a stool
in the door of her house, in the highest spot of the city, that
she may call to those passing by on the street and to the
people on their journey, 'Let anyone who is young turn in
here to me.' And she has said to the fool, 'Secret waters are
sweeter and hidden bread tastier.' And he does not know
that monsters are there and that her guests are in the depths
of hell,"[8] for whoever consorts with her descends into hell,
and whoever abstains from her will be made whole.

What colors, I ask you, could more vividly paint the allure-
ments of the envenomed flesh as it tempts the soul to the
squalor of sin, or the depravity of this flesh as it cries out
against spirit, or the miserable ruin when it conquers?

To sum up, then, spirit makes us godlike; the flesh, brutish.
The soul makes us men: spirit makes us good men, flesh
makes us vile men, but the soul in itself makes us neither
good nor bad. The spirit desires things celestial; the flesh,
things pleasurable; the soul, things related to it. The spirit
lifts us toward heaven, the flesh pushes us down toward hell,
the soul has neither power ascribed to her. Whatever is
carnal is base, whatever is spiritual is perfect, whatever is
soul is neutral—to be neither sought nor shunned.

Would you like, as the rather crude saying goes,[9] to have the distinction between these three parts pointed out to you, so to speak, by finger? Well, I will try. You esteem your parents, you love your brother and your children, you are fond of your friend. Now, doing these things is not so much a virtue as not doing them is abominable. Why should you, a Christian, not do what even pagans do by natural impulse —indeed, what mere beasts do? The natural action is not to be ascribed to merit. But suppose you have arrived at this situation, where either you must reject your feeling for father, suppress your love for your children, disregard your friend's goodwill—or offend God? Now what are you going to do? The soul stands at a fork in the road, with the flesh pulling one way and the spirit another.

"God is greater than parent," says the spirit. "To the one you owe only your body; to the other, everything."

"Unless you obey," says the flesh, "your father will disinherit you, people will call you unnatural. Think of the expedient; think of your reputation. God either is not watching your behavior, or He winks at it, or else He will surely be easily soothed."

Now the soul is perplexed and wavering. She inclines this way and that, and she will become whatever she yields to. If, rejecting the spirit she listens to the deceiving flesh, she becomes one with the body; but if, spurning the flesh she is elevated in the direction of the spirit, she will be transfigured into spirit.[10]

Get used to examining yourself closely in this manner, for it is the great error of mankind, not infrequently, to mistake the merely natural for absolute virtue. Certain passions— those outwardly rather respectable and masquerading, so to speak, as virtues—deceive the unthinking.

Suppose a judge gives short shrift to malefactors; he thinks of himself as a stern and incorruptible man. But would you care to look into him? If he is indulging his own disposition and yielding to a certain innate harshness, if he feels no distress of mind, but perhaps even a kind of pleasure, even though he never leaves off being a judge, then he should not be too highly pleased with himself. What he does is, morally, on a middle ground. If he is misusing the law for a private grudge or out of cupidity, then what he does is carnal and he is committing murder. But if he feels sharp grief of mind in being forced to destroy a man he would have preferred to reform and save, if he inflicts a merited punishment in the spirit of a father ordering his dearest son to be cut off and burned, then his action stems from the spiritual part.

Because of some natural inclination or peculiarity of temperament, most men take pleasure in some things and abhor others. There are people to whom sexual pleasure appeals not at all. These persons should not arrogate virtue to themselves for something which is a matter of indifference to them. Virtue lies, not in being incapable of sensuality, but in subduing it. One man delights in fasting, in attending mass, in going to church regularly, in reciting—though only from the mouth—as many Psalms as he can. Measure what he does by this rule: if he has an eye on public opinion or on profit, he smacks of the flesh, not the spirit. If he is only catering to his own bent—for he is doing what is agreeable to him—then he does, not what *should* especially delight him, but what he should be especially afraid of.

Here is your danger. You pray, and you condemn the man who does not pray. You fast, and you censure the man who eats.[11] Do you consider yourself better than someone who does not do the things you do? Take care that your fasting does not smack of carnality. Or suppose that a brother needs your help; you, in the meantime, mumble your prayers to God while you disregard your brother's need. God will turn His back on those prayers of yours, for how will the Lord hear your praying when you, a man, do not hear a fellow man? And listen to this: suppose you love your wife, but only because she is your wife in name. You do nothing extraordinary, for this you have in common even with the pagans. Or suppose you love her only because she provides you with sexual pleasure. Your love then is compatible only with the flesh. But if you love her most deeply because in her you have seen the likeness of Christ, that is to say, goodness, modesty, sobriety, chastity, and you love her now not in herself but in Christ, then in reality you love Christ in her; and so, at last, you love in a spiritual sense. But more about these matters in their proper place.

NINE

Certain General Rules for the True Christian Life

Now, SINCE WE seem somehow to have opened up a path toward our original goal and uncovered, as it were, a thicket of material, we must hurry on to the rest to prevent this becoming a bulky tome instead of a handy guidebook. We shall try, however, to pass on briefly certain rules—some wrestling holds, one might say—with the help of which you can easily extricate yourself from the labyrinthine errors of this world and, using these rules like the thread of Daedalus, find your way into the clear light of spiritual living. No discipline lacks its own guiding principles; will only the art of living happily, then, be assisted by having no such rules?

There is, unquestionably, a certain science or skill in virtuous living, and those who seriously train themselves in it are favored by that promoter of godly efforts, the spirit. On the other hand, those who say, "Leave us alone. We do not want to understand your ways,"[1] these men divine mercy will reject because they themselves have rejected understanding.

These rules will be concerned in part with the persons of God, Satan, and ourselves; in part with qualities, such as vices, virtues, and whatever is related to these qualities; in part with the sources or occasions of virtue and vice. They will be especially helpful in dealing with three evils which are the residue of original sin. For even if baptism has cleansed the stain, something of the old guilt still clings to us, left in us both as the guard of humility and the source or raw material of virtue. These evils are blindness, the flesh, and frailty.

Blindness clouds the mind's judgment with the fog of ignorance. Not only has the sin of our first parents somewhat dimmed that supremely clear radiance of the divine countenance which our Creator bestowed upon us; but also corrupt training, lewd company, perverse passion, the darkness of vice, and the habit of sin have so blighted it that the traces of God's law engraved there are scarcely discernible. So, as I started to say, blindness gives us faulty vision in our choice of things: it makes us follow the worst in place of the best, esteem what is more important less than what is convenient.

The flesh so provokes our passions that even if we know what is best we nevertheless love the opposite. Frailty brings it about that, overcome either by boredom or temptation, we abandon virtues which we once cultivated. Blindness affects our judgment, the flesh corrupts our will, and frailty undermines our constancy. It is more important, therefore, that you distinguish between what you ought to avoid and what you ought to seek; for that reason blindness must be cured if we are not to stumble about aimlessly in the making of choices.

The next point is to hate the evil, once you have recognized it, and to love the good; and here you must conquer the flesh or else, against the mind's better judgment, you will love what is merely pleasant rather than what is good for you. The third point is to persevere in courses well begun. For that reason you must put stiffening in your weakness to keep from leaving the path of virtue, a thing more disgraceful than never starting upon it. You must mend your ignorance to see where you ought to go, control your flesh so you will not stray from the discovered route into bypaths, and toughen your moral flabbiness so that, having started on the straight and narrow, you neither waver nor halt nor turn aside nor, having put your hand to the plow, look back,[2] but rejoice like a giant at the course to be run,[3] straining forward always toward those things ahead and forgetful of what is behind[4] until you seize the reward and crown promised to those who persevere.[5] To the best of our ability, therefore, we shall offer certain rules for accomplishing these three things.

TEN

Against the Sin of Ignorance: The First Rule (Faith)

SINCE FAITH IS really the sole approach to Christ, the first rule should be that you understand as clearly as possible about Him and about the Holy Scriptures handed down by His spirit and that you not entertain belief only by lip service —coldly, listlessly, hesistantly, as most Christians do—but let it permeate your whole being, let it be deeply and immovably fixed until there is not even an iota contained in Scripture that does not pertain to your spiritual well-being.

Do not let yourself be influenced by the fact that you see a sizable part of mankind living as if heaven and hell were old wives' tales, bugaboos, or children's games. Believe confidently and without haste. Even if the whole world should be unanimous in lunacy, even if the elements be turned topsy turvy or the angels revolt, Truth cannot lie. What God has prophesied must come to pass. If you believe He is God, you have to believe He is Truth. Maintain your confidence that nothing you hear with your own ears or see with your own eyes or grasp in your own hands is so true, nothing is so certain and unquestionable as that which you read in the Scripture. The authority of heaven—in other words, Truth—has inspired this, the holy prophets have revealed it, the blood of countless martyrs has affirmed it, the consensus of righteous men has for countless ages subscribed to it. While He was here in the flesh, Christ transmitted it in His words and expressed it in His character. Miracles attest it, and devils confess it—and even believe it so much that they tremble in fear.[1]

Finally, those things which are so harmonious with natural equity, which so agree with one another, so engage our attention, so move and transfigure us—if these telling marks of evidence fit only the Scripture, what damnable madness it is to be irresolute in faith! From past events you should conjecture the future: what extraordinary, incredible-sounding things did the prophets foretell about Christ! And which of these things has not come about? Will He who has not failed in those things fail in others? Last of all, if the prophets have not deceived us, will Christ, the Lord of prophets, deceive us?

If with these reflections and others of the same sort you fan the blaze of your faith from time to time and then pray fervently that God increase it, I will be surprised if you are able to be wicked very long. Who is so inexorably vicious that he would not recoil from his vices if only he believed deeply that with these transient pleasures he is purchasing—along with the wretched unhappiness of his conscious mind—eternal suffering as well? Or if, on the other hand, he believed that the righteous would be granted, in return for their trivial and fleeting little inconveniences, the hundred-fold joy of a clear conscience and, finally, everlasting life?

ELEVEN

The Second Rule (Action)

LET YOUR FIRST principle be, then, to have no doubt at all
about God's promises; and the next, to enter upon the way
of spiritual health, not slowly or timorously, but resolutely,
wholeheartedly, with a confident and—if I may use the expression—pugnacious spirit, ready to expend either your
goods or your life for Christ. The sluggard vacillates. The
kingdom of heaven is not won by indolence; plainly it takes
pleasure in meeting with strength.[1] Impetuous men grasp it.

Do not let your affection for loved ones delay your hasten-
ing to this destination; do not let the enticements of the world
call you away, or domestic cares hold you back. You must
strike off the chains of temporal affairs, since they cannot be
slackened. You must forsake Egypt in such a way as to prevent your ever returning in spirit to the flesh pots.[2] Speedily,
and once and for all, you must abandon Sodom and never
look back: the woman did this and was turned into an image
of stone.[3] The man has no leisure to loiter any place at all but
is ordered to hurry on to the mountain if he does not want
to perish.

The prophet enjoins us to flee from the midst of Babylon,[4]
and the departure from Egypt is called a flight. We are commanded to run away from Babylon, not to inch out of it by
degrees. You see most people floating aimlessly, without purpose, and with tactics too dilatory, undertaking to escape
from their vices.

"After I have freed myself from these troubles," they say,
or "After I have finished this or that piece of business."

Fool, what if your soul is required of you today?[5] Do you
not know that one piece of business is tied in with another?

That one vice leads to another? Rather, why not do today the thing which, as soon as you have done it, becomes easier by the doing?

And be attentive to another point: in this business, the headlong approach is the one most profitable. Do not ponder, do not weigh how much you are giving up. Christ alone will surely take the place of everything else. Dare to trust yourself to Him with all your heart; dare to distrust yourself; dare to transfer every care you have to Him. Stop relying upon yourself; cast yourself with complete confidence upon Him, and He will receive you. Turn your thoughts toward the Lord and He will support you[6] so that you can sing with the prophet: "The Lord rules over me and I will lack nothing. In a place of pasture, there has He placed me. He has raised me beside refreshing water; He transfigures my soul."[7]

Do not hope to divide yourself in two parts, one for the world and one for Christ. You cannot serve two masters.[8] God and Belial have no fellowship. The Master does not tolerate those who limp on both legs;[9] He spews out those people who are neither hot nor cold, but lukewarm. God is a very jealous lover of souls. He wants to possess alone and entirely that which He has redeemed by His blood.[10] He cannot abide any mutual sharing with Satan, whom He once subdued by His own death.

There are only two paths; the one which lies through indulgence of the passions leads to destruction; the other, proceeding through mortification of the flesh, leads to life.[11] What are you puzzled about? There is no third road: by one or the other, willy nilly you have to go. Whoever you are, you must enter this narrow path over which few men walk. This, however, is the one Christ Himself trod and the one which, from the dawn of creation, whoever has pleased God has taken.

This, surely, is the inescapable necessity of Adrasteian nemesis: [12] if you wish to live with Christ you must be cruci-

fied to the world with Christ.[13] Why do we delude ourselves
like fools? Why do we deceive ourselves in a matter so important? This man says, "I'm not a cleric, I'm a layman. It is
impossible for me not to make use of the world." Another
one thinks, "Even if I am a priest, I am not a monk. Let *him*
see to it." But the monk has also found a way of flattering
himself. "I," he says, "am not so straitlaced as this kind or
that kind." Someone else says, "I am a young man, I am a
nobleman, I am a rich man, I am a courtier, I am even a
prince. Words spoken to the apostles do not have anything to
do with me." Wretched man! Does it then mean nothing to
you to live in Christ? If you are in the world, you are not in
Christ.

Of course, everyone is in the world if by *world* you mean
sky, earth, sea, and this common air; but if by *world* you refer to pleasures, ambition, greed, sensuality, then assuredly
you are not a Christian if you are a worldling. Christ has told
everyone that whoever does not take up his own cross and
follow in His footsteps is not worthy of Him.[14] Dying with
Christ as far as the flesh is concerned means nothing to you
if living by His spirit means nothing. Being crucified to the
world means nothing if living with God means nothing. Being buried with Christ is nothing if being resurrected in glory
is nothing. The humility of Christ, His poverty, hardship,
scorn, labor, suffering, and grief are nothing to you if His
kingdom is nothing to you.

What is more shameful than to share a reward along with
the rest but to dump upon a certain few the exertions by
which the reward is won? And what is more irresponsible
than wanting to rule with the Head but being unwilling to
suffer with Him? Therefore, brother, do not look around at
what other people are doing and soothe yourself by comparison with them. Dying to sin, to fleshly desires, and to the
world is no easy matter, a fact appreciated by very few people, even monks. Nevertheless, this is the common profession

of all Christians. By what holier or more religious vow can one undertake anything? Either we must perish or, without exception, we must proceed by this road to salvation,

> whether we be kings
> Or penniless farmers.[15]

But if not everyone can attain to the perfect resemblance to our Head, at least we must all struggle in that direction with might and main. The man who has resolved with steadfast heart to become a Christian is already well on his way in the Christian life.

TWELVE

The Third Rule

(Despise Illusions; Choose the Way of Christ)

IN ORDER THAT you may not be put off from the path of righteousness by the fact that it seems hard and rough—partly because you must give up the pleasurable things of this world and partly because you have everlastingly to cope with three very wily foes in the flesh, the Devil, and the world—keep this third rule always in mind: like Vergil's Aeneas you should shrug off as nothing all the bogey men and fantasies which assail you, so to speak, in the very jaws of hell.[1] If you despise these empty illusions and scrutinize more carefully and steadily reality itself, you will surely see that no path is easier than the way of Christ, quite apart from the fact that it alone leads to felicity, and disregarding any prospect of reward.

What kind of worldly life can you choose, I ask you, in which there are not sorrows and difficulties in abundance to be suffered and endured? Who but the most ingenuous or foolish does not know that a courtier's life is full of trouble?

Good Lord! What a lasting and humiliating bondage one has to serve in these positions, how anxiously he has to curry favor with the prince, and court the goodwill of those who can help him or block his path. Over and over again he has to compose his face to suit the occasion and stomach the insults doled out by powerful men.

Again, what kind of evil can you name which the military life is not loaded with? (You can be your own best witness as to both kinds of life, since you have learned about both at your own peril.) Still again, what does the businessman not endure, "trying to escape ruin by sea, land, or fire."[2] What a burden of household cares, what vexations do those who try marriage find in it! How much trouble and work and risk in getting into public office! Look where you will, you see a vast swarm of fretful annoyances; mortal life itself is subject to a thousand ills common to just and unjust alike. Now, all of these things will turn into a mountain of benefits if they befall you while you are on the road to Christ; if you are not, they will be that much more distressing, that much more profitless, and yet must be endured.

Consider those who serve this world. In the first place, how many years they puff and sweat and strain, and for what fleeting bagatelles! Finally, with what dubious prospects! And add to this the fact that in the world there is no end at all to care and anxiety; the longer one has exerted himself, the more painfully he is troubled. Then what is the end at last of a life so bedeviled and distracted? Unquestionably, eternal punishment.

Now go and compare this life with the way of virtue, which is not difficult from the start and grows easier with practice, which becomes the delightful road that we travel with steadfast hope toward the highest good. Is it not absolute madness to prefer to purchase, at the same price, everlasting death rather than immortal life? But those people are acting even more demented who choose to go with the

grimmest travail to everlasting travail rather than with moderate effort toward endless tranquillity. Even if the path of
virtue were vastly more laborious than the way of the world,
nevertheless this harshness of effort would be softened by the
hope of reward, and we have that divine blessing which turns
all gall into honey. In the world care produces care, grief is
born of grief, there is no respite or quiet: all around a man,
labor and affliction; inside him, a more grievous sickness. The
very remedies make things worse.

Not even the pagan poets failed to make this appraisal of
the situation; in the punishments of Tityus, Ixion, Tantalus,
Sisyphus, Pentheus, they picture the calamitous life of wicked
men. Also to the point here is that belated confession in the
book of Sapience: "We have grown weary in the way of iniquity and destruction, we have walked hard roads, nor have
we known the path of the Lord."[3] What is more foul or laborious than slavery in Egypt? What is more melancholy than
captivity in Babylon? What is more intolerable than the yoke
of Pharaoh and Nebuchadnezzar? But what does Christ say?
"Put my yoke upon yourselves and you will find rest for your
souls, for my yoke is easy and my burden light."[4]

In sum, no pleasure is missing where a tranquil conscience
is present; no distress is absent where an uneasy conscience
is hurting. You ought to be more than convinced of this now,
but if you are doubtful, consult those who in times past have
turned to the Lord from out of the midst of Babylon, and
trust in their experience that nothing is more chaotic and unhappy than evil, nothing more commodious and delightful
than goodness.

But come now, suppose the wages and effort to be alike.
How much better, even so, to serve under the standards of
Christ than the banners of Satan. Indeed, how much better
to be knocked about with Christ than to swim in pleasures
with the Devil! Furthermore, should one not flee by horse
and sail from a master who is not only most abominable but

also most cruel and treacherous, who enforces a service so ruinous and extends promises so empty—but which still not infrequently take in deluded wretches?

Or suppose he make good his promises? Again, he exalts men when he pleases only that they may suffer much more at losing what they have so arduously gained. After a merchant has blurred out the distinctions between right and wrong in his passion to accumulate property, after he has exposed his reputation, his life, his soul to a thousand perils—even if the die of fortune has rolled luckily for him, what has he concocted for himself but an occasion for anxious care if he keeps his wealth, or torture if he loses it? But if the die falls unluckily, what is left for him except to become twice miserable, once because he was frustrated in getting what he hoped for and, again, because he cannot think without sorrow of such an expense of wasted effort.

No one has pressed on with fixed purpose toward soundness of understanding without achieving it. Just as Christ will not be mocked, by the same token He will not mock us.[5] Reflect that when you flee from the world to Christ, you do not give up anything—if the world has any advantages—but are exchanging trifles for things of importance. Who would not gladly exchange silver for gold, a stone for a gem? If your friends are offended, what of it? You will find more agreeable ones. You will be deprived of pleasures, will you? You will enjoy inward satisfactions sweeter, cleaner, and more certain. You must share your material goods? You will increase in those riches which neither moths destroy nor thieves carry off.[6] You will no longer be important among worldlings? But you have the stamp of approval from Christ, your Creator. You please fewer men? Better ones, though. Your body grows lean, but your soul feasts. Your external sleekness diminishes, but your spiritual comeliness becomes luminous.

And if you will run through the other aspects in this same way, you will find that everyone of these seeming goods to be abandoned in this world is replaced by something of far greater value. Suppose, however, that there are things which, though they cannot be *desired* without sin, can nevertheless be possessed without it: of this sort would be popular esteem, the goodwill of the people, favor, authority, friends, the honor virtue commands. Now, it commonly happens that those who seek first the kingdom of God are given all these things gratuitously.[7] This is what Christ has promised, and what God did for Solomon.[8] Fortune often pursues those who run from it and runs from those who pursue it. Certainly, whatever happens to those who love God, nothing can be unpropitious to one for whom loss is turned into gain, scourging into comfort, insults into glory, pain into pleasure, grief into sweetness, evil into good.[9]

Do you hesitate, then, to enter upon this journey and to give up that other one, when you have comparisons so disparate—better to say, nonexistent—as God with Satan, hope with hope, reward with reward, hardship with hardship, comfort with comfort?

THIRTEEN

The Fourth Rule

(Christ as the Only Goal)

BUT IN ORDER that you may press forward to felicity by a more trustworthy course, take this as your fourth rule: that you set Christ before you as the only goal of your whole life and direct all your efforts, all your activities, all your leisure, all your business in His direction. Think of Christ, not as an empty word, but as nothing other than love, candor, patience, purity—in brief, whatever He taught. Think of the Devil as nothing but whatever things call us away from those qualities. A man impelled toward virtue alone is turning to-

ward Christ; a man serving his own vices is surrendering to
Satan. Let your eye be clear, therefore, and your whole being
will be full of light.[1] Look at Christ alone as the absolute
Good, so that you may love nothing, marvel at nothing, want
nothing but Christ or because of Christ; and hate nothing,
despise nothing, shun nothing except wickedness or because
of wickedness.

Thus it will come about that whatever you do, whether
you are asleep or awake, eating or drinking, even in your
very sports and pastimes[2]—I will go so far as to include even
certain of the lesser frailties we sometimes fall into as we hasten toward virtue—all of these things will be translated for
you into a mountain of rewards. But if your eye is going to
be misdirected and look elsewhere than at Christ, then, even
if you have acted with propriety, your deeds will be barren
or even injurious.[3] For it is a fault to do even a good deed for
the wrong reason.

Therefore, whatever you encounter on the road as you
press forward toward the goal of the supreme Good, that you
must reject or accept solely to the extent that it hinders or
helps your journey. In general, these contingencies may be
grouped in three categories:

Some things—avenging an injury, for example, or bearing
malice toward another man—are so abominable that they
can never be honorable. These actions or conditions you
must always spurn, no matter what suffering or exertion you
incur in doing so, for nothing whatever can harm a good man
except his own vile practices.

At the other extreme are certain qualities so inherently fine
that they cannot be culpable, such as wishing everyone well,
helping one's friends by honorable means, hating evil, taking
pleasure in edifying conversation.

And some things—health, good looks, energy, eloquence,
learning, and the like—occupy a neutral ground. Of this last
category, therefore, one should pursue none for its own sake,

nor should he rely upon them any more or less than they help him hit the final mark.

To the philosophers certain goals are incomplete and indecisive; we should not rest in them. It is all very well to make use of them but not to settle down to enjoy them. And not all of these neutral qualities are, of course, equally helpful or obstructive to those who are moving toward Christ. They must be taken up or rejected, therefore, according to the extent they serve the purpose. Knowledge is of greater use to the good life than beauty or bodily strength or money, and although all learning can be made relevant to Christ, one kind is more directly helpful than another.

You should measure the usefulness, or uselessness, of all these indecisive resources in terms of this end. You love learning: that's fine—if you love it for the sake of Christ. But if you love it only that you may have knowledge, then you are coming to rest in a place where you should have made a step forward. But if you thirst for scholarship so that with its help you may more clearly understand the Christ permeating the mysteries of Scripture and may love Him when you understand Him and share or enjoy Him when you have thus loved and understood Him—in that case, apply yourself to the acquisition of learning, but not beyond the point where you think it will contribute to that sound understanding. If you trust yourself and hope for great profit in Christ, press on like a bold merchant to travel even further into the literature of the pagans and convert the riches of Egypt to the adornment of the Lord's temple. But if you are more afraid of the cost than hopeful of gain, come back to that first rule: know yourself, and be reconciled to your own limitations. It is better to know less and love more than to know a great deal and love not at all.

Knowledge, then, holds first place among the attributes of this middle group; after that come health, natural talents, eloquence, appearance, strength, rank, favor, authority, prosperity, reputation, family, friends, domestic property. To the extent that any one of these things assists us to virtue by the nearest route, to that extent we ought to cultivate it especially, but only if it presents itself to us as we are pushing on in that direction. Otherwise, we should not turn aside for their sake from the course we have set. If money falls to your lot without offering any impediment to a sound sense of values, use it: out of this Mammon of wickedness make friends for yourself. But if you are afraid you will lose peace of mind, then scorn this pernicious wealth; imitate that Crates of Thebes[4] and hurl the offending burden into the sea rather than impede your way to Christ. This will be easier for you to do if, as we have said, you get in the habit of being impressed by nothing extraneous to yourself, that is, the things which have nothing to do with the inward man. In this way it will come about that you neither become puffed up if these things fall to your lot nor dispirited if they should be denied you or taken from you. Obviously, you are to measure your well-being in terms of Christ alone.

If, however, they should come to you without effort on your part, you should be more concerned, not more complacent. Look at the situation this way: you have, by God's will, been given a means of expressing virtue, but a dangerous one. And if you regard with suspicion the benign look of fortune, do as Prometheus did.[5] Decline the treacherous box and hurry on, free and unimpeded, toward that one and only Good. Indeed, those who with anxious care seek money as if it were something important, who see in it the chief support of life, who consider themselves happy as long as it is safe and bewail their bad luck when it is lost—these people surely have fashioned too many gods for themselves. If money can make you happy or unhappy, you have made it the equal of Christ.

And what I have said about money is also true of official dignities, of pleasures, of good health, indeed of mortal life

itself. One needs to be working with such wholehearted conviction toward Christ alone that he has no time to care
greatly about any of these things, whether they are given
him or taken away from him. For the time is brief, as the
Apostle says: "From now on let those who deal with this
world be as though they had no dealings with it."[6]

This attitude, I know, the world will jeer at as folly and
madness, but only by means of this folly has it pleased God
to save those who believe in Him. And the foolishness of God
is wiser than men.[7]

Whatever you do, therefore, you should weigh by this rule.
You train yourself in a certain skill; very good, if you do it
honestly. But what end do you have in view? That you may
support your family? But to what end do you support your
family? That you may make it useful to Christ? You are
pressing forward as you should. Or suppose that you are fasting, a pious performance it would seem. But what is the purpose of your fasting? That you may abstain from food? That
you may be considered the more devout? Your vision is corrupted.[8]

But suppose you fast to keep from getting sick. Why do
you fear sickness? Because it would keep you from enjoying
sensual pleasures? Your vision is very faulty. Then suppose
you wish to stay well so that you may keep up in your studies. Now these studies—where are you directing them? Toward getting some priestly office? But with what intentions
do you court this office? Why, that you may live for yourself,
not for Christ. You have strayed, then, from the standard
which a Christian ought always to hold before him.

On the other hand, suppose you eat food to make yourself
physically strong, but you want to be strong so that you can
sustain your devotional pursuits and prayerful vigils. In that
case you have hit the mark. But if you are careful about your
health so that you will not lose your good looks or your sexual prowess, you have lost touch with Christ and made another god for yourself.

Some men worship certain saints with certain rites.[9] One fellow pays his respects to Christopher every day, but only in the presence of the saint's statue. What is he eyeing? Obviously this: he has persuaded himself that for that day he will be safe from the death he dreads. Another prays to a certain Roch, but why? Because he thinks that saint protects the body from the plague. Still another mumbles certain prayers to Barbara or to George lest he fall into the hands of his enemies. This fellow fasts in deference to Apollonia so that his teeth will not ache. That one looks at images of godly Job in order to avoid the itch. Some offer a certain portion of their money to the poor to keep from losing their goods in shipwreck, or they burn a little candle in front of Jerome to effect the recovery of lost property.[10]

In fine, the number of things we either fear or hope for is matched, according to this program, by the number of saints we put in charge of those things. And these saints themselves vary with different nations. Paul, for example, is a favorite with the French for the same purposes that Jerome is among our own countrymen; and the things James or John perform in this place or in that neither can perform everywhere.

Now, unless this kind of worship is restored to Christ and detached from any consideration of creature comforts or inconveniences, it is actually not Christian at all. It is not much different from the superstition of those who in earlier times used to promise Hercules a tenth of their goods in the hope that they might get rich, or offer a cock to Aesculapius that they might recover from an illness, or slaughter a bull to Neptune that they might have a safe voyage. The names have been changed, of course, but the purpose is the same.

You pray God that you may not die too soon, not that He may bountifully give you sounder judgment and that wherever death takes you it may not catch you unprepared. You are not considering how you may change your life, and yet you petition God not to let you die. Then what are you asking? Clearly that you may go on sinning as long as possible.

You pray for riches, but you do not know how to make use
of them. Are you not praying for your own ruin? You beg
for good health, but you abuse it. Is not your "piety" an im-
piety?

At this point certain religionists will straightway protest—
those who think money-making is synonymous with virtue[11]
and, as Paul also says, "seduce the minds of the unsophisti-
cated with certain soothing benisons, obedient to their own
bellies rather than to Jesus Christ."[12] Will they not say, then,
"Do you forbid the worship of saints, in worshiping whom
you worship God?"

As a matter of fact, I do not so much censure those who do
these things out of a kind of ingenuous superstition as I do
those who, with an eye to their own profit, parade certain observances, which may perhaps be tolerable, as if they represented the highest and purest devotion, and for their own
gain encourage the ignorance of the common people, of
which not even I am entirely critical. I will not endure this
substitution of the mediocre for the best, of the least important for the most. I will approve of their asking that Roch of
theirs for life and safety if they consecrate that life to Christ,
but I will praise them more if they pray for nothing but an increased hatred of vice and a burgeoning love of virtue. As
for living and dying, let them consign these matters to the
hands of God and say with Paul, "Whether we live or die, we
live and die in the Lord."[13] It will be a perfect thing if they
wish to depart and be with Christ;[14] if they find their glory
and joy in sickness, in injury, and in the other adversities of
fortune. Those are held worthy who in this way are shaped
to resemble their Head.

To do things of this sort, therefore, is not so blameworthy
as it is destructive to come to a halt with them and to lean
upon them. I allow the infirmity, but like Paul I point out a
better way.[15] If you will scrutinize all your efforts and actions in the light of this rule and never bog down in these

halfway measures before you have come at last all the way
to Christ, you will neither stray away from the path at any
time nor do or suffer anything in life which may not be converted into ingredients of religious devotion.

FOURTEEN

The Fifth Rule

(From the Visible to the Invisible;
The Way to a Pure and Spiritual Life)

As a buttress, so to speak, to this rule let us add a fifth, so
that you may evaluate perfect piety by this one principle:
in accordance with that division of man presented earlier,
you should always try to advance from things visible, which
are for the most part imperfect or of a neutral status, to things
invisible. This precept is so pertinent to the matter that when
they either neglect it or do not understand it, most Christians
are merely full of credulous wonder, not devout, and except
for using the *name* of Christ are not far removed from the
superstition of pagans.

Let us picture to ourselves, then, two kinds of worlds: one
accessible only to the understanding, the other to the sight.
The intelligible world, which we may call the angelic, is the
one in which God dwells with the most blessed minds. The
visible is made up of the heavenly spheres and whatever is
included in them. Then let us think of man as a kind of third
world, sharing in each of the others—visible as to body, invisible as to soul. Because we are aliens in this visible world,
it behooves us never to be idle, but by means of some appropriate analogy, to refer whatever assaults our senses either
to the spiritual world or—a more serviceable procedure—
to ethical values and that part of man which corresponds to
the spiritual world. What this visible sun is to the visible

world, the celestial Mind is to the intelligible world and to that part of you which corresponds to it, namely, the spirit. What the moon there is to the one world, the society of angels and blessed souls which we call the Church Triumphant is to the other, and this the spirit is in you.

Whatever role the higher world plays on the earth beneath it, this function God has in your soul. The sun sets, rises, grows hot, becomes milder, inspires life, engenders, ripens, attracts, refines, cleanses, hardens, softens, illuminates, quiets, exhilarates. Therefore, whatever you see in the sun, indeed whatever you see in this grosser world of the elements which many have considered as distinct from the rest of the universe, and finally whatever exists in the grosser part of yourself—all these things you should get in the habit of relating to God and to the invisible part of yourself.

So it will come about that anything presenting itself to the senses at any time will become for you an occasion of righteousness. When this visible sun daily refreshes your physical eyes as it bathes the earth with new light, think immediately of what bliss exists in heaven, where that eternal Sun is always on high and never sets; and think how great is that joy of a pure mind illuminated by the radiance of God. And, instructed by visible creation, pray with Paul that He who ordered the light to shine out of darkness may Himself shine in your heart to give the light of the knowledge of the glory of God in the face of Christ Jesus.[1] Recollect similar places in the Holy Scriptures where here and there the grace of the Holy Spirit is compared to light. If night seems dark and foreboding to you, imagine a soul deprived of divine radiance and darkened by sin. And if you detect any night within yourself, pray that the sun of righteousness may rise for you.[2]

Think of this, too: that compared to things unseen the objects of the visible world present to the eyes nothing more than insubstantial copies of those realities. Just as whatever you perceive in the material realm either attracts or repels you, so it will follow that in this inward world the spirit will love or detest some things far more than others. If physical beauty is pleasing to the eye, think how splendid is beauty of soul. If an ugly face seems disagreeable, remember how odious is a mind steeped in vice.

Go through this same process with the rest of the correspondences. For just as the soul has its own beauty or foulness, with which it respectively pleases God or Satan, like unto like, so it also has its own youth, senility, sickness, health, death, life, poverty, affluence, pleasure, grief, war, peace, cold, heat, thirst, drink, hunger, food. In short, whatever is sensorily experienced in the body should be understood of the soul.

Here then lies the way to a pure and spiritual life: to gradually accustom ourselves to being alienated from those things which in reality are illusory but which sometimes seem to be what they are not—gross sensuality, for instance, and worldly glory—and which pass away and quickly melt into nothingness; and then to be ravished by those things which are truly lasting, immutable, and true. This Socrates understood, a philosopher not so much in his talk as in his living. He says that at length the soul gladly departs from the body if, through the love of wisdom, it has already thought earnestly about death and has also, long before the event, accustomed itself, so to speak, to part company with the body by despising material forms and loving and contemplating the spiritual.[3]

This is the only Cross to which Christ has called us,[4] and the only death in which Paul wants us to die in company with our Head.[5] The prophet also has this to say: "For Your sake we are slain all day long; we have been counted like sheep for the slaughter."[6] And the Apostle puts it in different terms: "We should seek those things which are above, not on earth. We should set our minds on those things which are on high."[7]

Their meaning is simply this: we should become foolish

in material matters and rendered insensible to them, so that the more inept we are in those affairs, the more discerning we may become in these of the spirit; the less we live outwardly, the more truly we begin to live inwardly. Finally, to put it more clearly, the less we are influenced by transitory considerations, the better we have become acquainted with the eternal; the less impressed we are by shadows, the more regard we have begun to have for reality.

This rule, therefore, we should always keep at hand, never to come to a standstill anywhere in temporary gratifications, but by the process of analogies ascend from that stage step by step, as it were, to the love of the spiritual—or at any rate begin to reject the visible world in favor of the world unseen. Sickness of the body will be more endurable if you think of it as medicine for the soul. You will be less anxious about your physical health if you give all your attention to guarding your mental health. If death of the body appalls you, death of the soul is much more appalling. If you shudder at the poison you can see because it produces bodily harm, you should shudder far more violently at the venom which destroys the soul. Hemlock is mischief to the body, but sensuality is a far worse bane to the soul. You tremble and turn pale at the thought of being struck by the lightning flashing from the clouds, but how much more you should fear that the invisible bolt of God's wrath will fall upon you: "Go, you accursed ones, into the everlasting fire."[8]

If physical beauty charms you, why are you not burning all the more hotly for that beauty which lies within? Transfer your love to something permanent, something celestial, something incorruptible, and you will love more coolly this transitory and fleeting form of the body. You pray that your fields may have rain so that they will not dry up; pray all the more fervently that God may refresh your mind with His showers to prevent its growing barren of the fruit of virtue. With great pains you make up the loss of money; with greater

pains you should repair any damage to the mind. You are
provident with regard to your old age, for fear you will lack
some bodily comfort; should you not see to it that spiritual
comforts are also not lacking? This process should be
adopted in dealing with all those matters which are daily apparent to our senses and which affect them variously—de-
pending upon the kind of impact—with hope, fear, love, hatred, grief, or pleasure.

Furthermore, you should observe in all your reading those
things consisting of both a surface meaning and a hidden
one—comparable to body and spirit—so that, indifferent to
the merely literal sense, you may examine most keenly the
hidden. Of this sort are the works of all the poets and of the
Platonists in philosophy. But especially do the Holy Scriptures, like the Silenus of Alcibiades,[9] conceal their real divinity beneath a surface that is crude and almost laughable.

Otherwise, if you read without allegorical interpretation
the account of Adam's being moulded out of damp earth
and having a soul breathed into him, of Eve shaped from an
extracted rib, of their being forbidden to eat of the tree, of
the wily Serpent, and of God strolling about to take the air,
of the guilty pair lying hidden, of the angel stationed at the
gate of Paradise with a turning sword to prevent their return
after they had been cast out[10]—in short, if in the whole story
of the creation you should look for nothing beyond the literal
and the superficial, I do not see that you would be doing anything much more worth the effort than if you were to sing
about the clay image made by Prometheus and how fire,
stolen by a trick and laid on the image, put life into the mud.

As a matter of fact, a poetic tale read allegorically may perhaps be more fruitful than an account from the sacred books
where you content yourself with only the rind. If, when you
read the myth of the Giants,[11] it teaches you that you should
not defy the gods or that you should shy away from those
practices abhorrent to nature, that your mind should be fixed

on those things—assuming that they are honorable—which you are by nature well fitted for, that you should not burden yourself with marriage if celibacy is more consonant with your character, or, conversely, that you should not undertake celibacy if marriage seems to fit you better (for as a rule things turn out badly when you try them in defiance of common sense); if the cups of Circe[12] teach you that men are crazed by sensuality as if it were sorcery and are promptly turned from men into beasts; if thirsting Tantalus shows you that one is most wretched when gazing hungrily at heaped up riches he does not dare to use; if the rock of Sisyphus convinces you that ambition is troubled and harassed, if the labors of Hercules show you that you achieve heaven by honest effort and tireless industry—are you not learning by means of fable the precepts offered by philosophers and divines as authorities on how to live?

On the other hand, if you should read of the infants contesting with each other in the womb, of the birthright sold for a mess of pottage, of a father's blessing preempted by trickery,[13] of Goliath struck down by David's slingshot,[14] of Samson's shaven hair[15]—without allegory it means less than if you were to read some poetical fiction. What does it matter whether you study the books of Kings or Judges, or the history of Livy, if you look at the veiled meaning in neither? In the history are many things which may improve general morals; in the other there are some things downright absurd, taken literally, and if understood only at the surface level, detrimental to morality. Consider, for example, the villainy of David—adultery procured by murder[16] —Samson's desperate infatuation, the clandestine coupling of Lot with his daughters,[17] and a thousand other instances of this kind.

Therefore, disregarding the mere skin of the Scripture, especially of the Old Testament, you will profit most from searching into its mystical spirit. In this way manna will have for you whatever taste you will have brought to it in your

own palate. In unveiling the hidden sense, however, one
ought not to follow conjectures of his own mind but acquire
a method and, so to speak, a kind of technique, something a
certain Dionysius[18] gives us in a book called *Concerning the
Names of God* and Saint Augustine in his work entitled
Christian Doctrine. After Christ, the Apostle Paul opened up
certain allegorical fountains; and following him, Origen easily holds the leadership in this aspect of theology.

Our divines, however, either spurn it altogether or handle
it in a very insipid fashion. Although in subtlety of disputa-
tion they equal or surpass the early writers, in their treatment
of this art they are not even to be compared with those men.[19]

As I see it, there are two principal reasons for this: for one
thing, it is impossible for the mystical sense not to be dull or
trivial when it is not seasoned with skill in eloquence and a
certain charm of language, something the older divines ex-
celled in but which we do not even approach. For another
thing, present-day theologians, devoted solely to Aristotle,
shut out the Platonists and Pythagoreans from the schools;
but these latter philosophers Augustine prefers,[20] not only
because they hold a great many views fully harmonious with
our religion, but also because their very manner of using a
language figurative and, as I have said, appropriate to allegory, comes closer to the style of the Holy Scriptures. So it is
not to be wondered at that theological allegory was handled
more perceptively and that, by their copiousness of language, any subject you please, even one dry and commonplace could be enriched and made attractive by those who
were the most learned men of all antiquity and who had already practiced on the books of Plato and the poets the skill
which they were to exercise later on in the interpretation of
holy mysteries.

I recommend, therefore, that you study the commentar-
ies of these men, for I want to instruct you, not in scholastic
quibbling, but in good living. However, if you do not pene-

trate to the hidden sense, remember at least that it lurks there; for it is better, certainly, to hope for something unattained than to rest supinely in the deadening letter. This is true not only of the Old Testament but also of the New. The Gospel has its own flesh, its own spirit.[21] Even if the veil has been drawn from the face of Moses, Paul is as yet seen through a glass darkly.[22] As Christ Himself has said in the Gospel of John: "The flesh accomplishes nothing; it is the spirit that gives life."[23] I must admit that if I had had the responsibility of saying that the flesh accomplishes nothing, it would have been enough for me to say that it does accomplish something, but the spirit much more. Now, however, Truth itself has spoken: "It accomplishes nothing." And according to Paul it is so ineffectual that unless it is brought back to the spirit it is deadly.[24]

In another sense the flesh has its value in that, by a kind of gradual process, it draws our weakness toward spirituality. Without the spirit the body cannot exist, but the spirit needs nothing from the body. If in Christ's teachings spirit is so important that it alone gives us life, we must strive to reach the point where in all our studies and in all our deeds we are mindful of the spirit rather than the flesh. And if one looked closely, he would see that this alone is the point to which we are called, among the prophets by Isaiah, and among the Apostles by Paul, who in virtually every epistle teaches and insists that nothing carnal can be trusted, that only in the spirit are life and freedom and light and adoption and those other desirable fruits he names. Everywhere he rejects, despises, and resists the flesh.

If you look carefully, you will find our Master, Jesus, teaching the same lesson in various places: in the references to pulling an ass from a pit,[25] restoring a blind man's sight,[26] rubbing together the ears of grain,[27] unwashed hands,[28] the feasts of sinners,[29] in the parable of the pharisee and the publican,[30] in passages dealing with fastings, the brothers according to the flesh,[31] the vainglory of the Jews in being descendants of Abraham,[32] the offering of gifts, praying, the enlargement of phylacteries,[33] and in many similar instances where He attacks the flesh of the law and the credulity of those who prefer to be Jews in outward show rather than inward truth.

And He makes the same point when He says to the woman of Samaria: "Woman, believe me: the hour comes when you will worship neither upon this mountain nor in Jerusalem, but the hour comes, and is now upon us, when the true worshippers will worship the Father in spirit and in truth. For the Father seeks such as honor Him; God is Spirit, and those who worship Him must worship in spirit and in truth."[34] He signified the same thing in His acts when at a wedding, He turned the water of the cold and insipid letter into the wine of spirituality,[35] thus making spiritual souls drunk even to the point of a disregard for life.

And lest you think it strange that Christ rejected these things we have just now been mentioning, He has even scorned the eating of His flesh and the drinking of His blood unless they are taken in a spiritual sense. Whom do you think He was talking to when He said that the flesh accomplishes nothing, that it is the spirit which quickens?[36] Certainly not to those people who think that if they have a copy of the Gospel or a copper cross hanging from their necks they are immune to every evil and that this is the perfect form of worship, but to those to whom He had disclosed the deepest significance of the eating of His Body. If so great a ritual is nothing—what is more, even dangerous—why should we put our confidence in any other carnal ceremony unless the spirit is present there?

It is possible that you say mass every day but live selfishly, untouched by the misfortunes of your neighbors. As yet you are still in the fleshly stage of the sacrament. But if you take to heart what the mass really stands for when you receive it, that is, being one spirit with the spirit of Christ, one body with the body of Christ, a living member of the Church; if you love nothing except in Christ; if you think all your property belongs equally to all men; if the trials of other people grieve you as much as your own—in that case you are at last observing the sacraments with real profit, because you are doing it in a spiritual sense. If you perceive that you are somehow transfigured in Christ and are living less and less in yourself, give thanks to the spirit which alone gives life. Many people are in the habit of counting up the number of masses they have attended each day and relying upon this practice as if it were of supreme importance, as if they owe Christ nothing more than this. Then, as soon as they get out of the church, they return to their old habits. I give them credit for their embracing the flesh of devoutness, but I cannot praise them for being content with that.

Let the thing visually represented—the death of your Lord—be experienced within yourself. Examine yourself and, as the saying goes, look into your heart; see how close you are to being dead to the world.[37] For if you are still wholly possessed by wrath, ambition, greed, lust, envy—then even if you are touching the very altar, you are still far from the sacrament. Christ died for you; you, then, should kill your own beastliness. Sacrifice yourself to Him who offered Himself to the Father for your sake. If you do not think of these things and put your faith in Him, God despises your smug and gross religion. You have been baptised, but do not for that reason suppose yourself forthwith a Christian. If your whole mind smacks of nothing but the world, you are a Christian only in the eyes of the world, but in reality more heathenish than the heathen. Why? Because you grasp at the body of the sacrament but are empty of the spirit.

What does it matter that your body has been washed, as long as your mind stays filthy? Suppose that your flesh has been sprinkled with salt; what of it, if mentally you remain

unsavory? What if the body has been anointed with oil, if
the soul is without that unction? But if you have been buried
spiritually with Christ and intend to walk with Him now in
newness of life, I acknowledge you as a Christian.[38] What
point is there in your being showered with holy water if you
do not wipe away the inward pollution from your heart? You
venerate the saints and delight in touching their relics, but
you despise the best one they left behind, the example of a
holy life.

No worship is more pleasing to Mary than emulation of
her humility, no religious veneration more acceptable, or
more appropriate, to the saints than trying to copy their virtues. You want to earn the favor of Peter and Paul, do you?
Then adopt the faith of the one and the charity of the other,
and you will have done better than if you run ten times
around Rome. You want to honor Saint Francis in the best
possible way? You are arrogant, you are a lover of money,
you are factious. Let your gift to the Saint be this: that you
curb your passions and, like Francis, be more humble; that
you despise filthy gain and prize spiritual riches instead; that
you give up quarreling and overcome evil with good. The
Saint will treat that as a much greater honor than your burning a hundred candles before him.[39]

You think it is a great thing, do you, to be swathed in a
Franciscan cowl when you are buried? If your character in
life was unlike that of Francis, wearing the same kind of
clothing in death will not do you any good. And, although
the exemplar of all goodness is sought most fittingly in Christ
Himself, yet if the worship of Christ in the person of His
saints pleases you so much, see to it that you imitate Christ
in the saints and for the honor of every one of them work
to remove every vice you have or to embrace every virtue.
If this happens, I will not censure those things which are
done for show.

I do not criticize your honoring the ashes of Paul if your

religion is firmly resolved, but if you venerate dumb, lifeless ashes[40] and at the same time neglect the image still living, speaking, and breathing, so to speak, in what he wrote,
is your religion not the reverse of what it should be? You
worship the bones of Paul hidden away in caskets, but not
the spirit of Paul permeating his teaching. You make much
of his body visible through glass, but you think nothing of
the whole mind of Paul resplendent in his words. You worship the dust before which, sometimes, bodily deformities
are removed; why not reverence even more the words by
which spiritual blemishes are healed? Let those faithful people for whom such signs are provided marvel at them. For
your part, as a man of faith who does not doubt that God can
do anything, embrace His books that you may learn to love
Him above everything else.

You honor a likeness of Christ's face that has been crudely
shaped out of rock or wood, or else daubed in paint; much
more to be honored is that likeness of His mind which, by
the working of the Holy Spirit, has been portrayed in the
words of the Gospels. No Apelles has ever painted the fea-
tures and figure of the body in the revealing way that the
image of the mind comes out in a man's speech, especially
in that of Christ who, since He was absolute simplicity and
truth, allowed no jarring note at all to mar the resemblance
between the archetype of the Divine Spirit and the likeness
of it described in His words.

Just as nothing is more like the Father than the Son, who is
the Word of the Father distilled from His inmost heart, so
nothing is more like Christ than the word of Christ uttered
from the inmost recesses of that most holy breast. And you do
not marvel at this likeness? You do not worship it? You do
not study it devoutly and embrace it in your heart? You have
relics so holy and so powerful of your Lord, and you neglect
these to seek things much less profitable?

Do you gape with awe at a robe or a handkerchief of Christ
and then have trouble staying awake when you read what

He said? You consider it vastly important to have at home
a little fragment of the Cross, but that possession amounts
to nothing in comparison to this other, that you carry the
mystery of the Cross deep within your heart. If such things
as that makes one holy, who was holier than the Jews, many
of the worst of whom saw Jesus with their own eyes when He
was living in the flesh, heard Him with their own ears and
touched Him with their own hands? Who, for that matter,
was luckier than Judas, who kissed the divine mouth with
his own? Without the spirit flesh is worth so little that it
would have done the Virgin Mother no good to have borne
Christ in her own body had she not received His spirit
through the Holy Spirit.

This is very important, but listen to something even more
important. While the Apostles were enjoying the bodily
presence of Christ in intimate companionship, do you not
read how vacillating they were, how slow to understand
Him? Who would want anything more perfect for spiritual
health than his long association with One who was both God
and man? And yet, after the performance of so many miracles, after years of teaching straight from His holy lips, after so many evidences of His resurrection, did He not at the
final moment when He was to be received into heaven chide
them for their lack of faith?[41] Then what was the reason? Assuredly the flesh of Christ stood in the way. So it is that He
says, "Unless I go away the Comforter will not come. It is
best for you that I go."[42]

The physical presence of Christ is useless as far as spiritual
health is concerned; shall we dare, then, to attribute such
perfect goodness to the possession of any other physical object? Paul had seen Christ in the flesh. What do you consider
more important than this? But he is indifferent to the fact.
"Even if we have known Christ in the flesh," he says, "we
know Him no longer."[43] Why not? Because he had achieved
more satisfying gifts of the spirit.

Perhaps I am arguing this point more lengthily than befits

one who is handing down rules; but I do this rather deliberately, and not without real occasion, because I consider it self-evident that this error is the common plague of all Christendom and inflicts a damage all the more pernicious for its looking so very much like piety. No sins are more dangerous than those which have the appearance of virtue. Apart from the fact that a slip is easy here even for good men, nothing is harder to correct, for the ignorant masses believe that religion is being profaned whenever behavior of this sort is censured. But let the whole world instantly clamor against you. Let certain loud-mouthed rabble rousers bluster, who gladly preach such things as those out of self-interest, keeping an eye upon their own profit, obviously, not upon Christ.

On account of either the ignorant credulity of these people or their pretended holiness, I often have to make it clear that I am not in any way criticizing the outward show of Christian observances or the zeal of simple folk, especially in those matters which have been sanctioned by the authority of the Church. Some of these ceremonies are at once the evidence and the support of piety. Since they are rather important to the infants in Christ, until they grow up and mature into full manhood,[44] it is not fitting even for adults in the faith to disdain them, lest they injure the weak by their example. I approve what you do if only the end is valid, if you are not content to stop at a place you should be treating as a stepping stone to something more important to spiritual health. But to worship Christ in visible ceremonies[45] and for the sake of material considerations, and to pin the value of religion upon these ceremonies, to be smug about oneself for this reason and to damn everybody else, to become obsessed by these things and even to linger in them and—to put it briefly—be diverted *from* Christ by those very practices He intended to lead us *to* Him—this is surely a departure from the law of the Gospel, which is spiritual, and a reduction to a kind of Judaism perhaps no less perilous than having to contend, minus this superstition, with powerful and manifest vices of the mind. The latter sickness is more deadly, true, but the other is harder to cure.

How valiantly did Paul, that advocate-extraordinary of things spiritual, work to draw the Jews, misled by their reliance upon ritualism, toward those things which pertain to the spirit! And now I see the general run of Christians falling back into that same error. But why did I say "the general run"? One might endure that, if only this same error had not seized upon a large part of the clergy, the learned, and, in fine, virtually the whole flock of those who in their speech and habits make a profession of the spiritual life. If the salt has lost its flavor, where will others get their seasoning?[46]

I am ashamed to report how gullibly most of those people look upon certain mere ceremonies, invented by little men, but not for such purposes, and how odiously they press these ceremonies upon others, how confidently they rely upon them, how boldly they judge other men, how belligerently they eye them. They think they deserve heaven for their punctiliousness in these matters where, once they have hardened in the routine, they consider themselves veritable Pauls and Antonys.[47] They begin with great superciliousness to exercise the office of censor upon any other kind of life, after the manner of fools, as the comic poet says, who think nothing right except what they themselves do.[48]

In spite of which, when they grow old in this business you will see them still smacking of the Christlike in nothing at all, but beastly and sodden with certain melancholy vices: peevish in companionship, hardly endurable even to themselves, cold in charity, hot in anger, stubborn in hatred, poisonous of tongue, inexorable in nursing a grudge, prepared to battle for trifles on any point you please, and therefore so alien to the perfection of Christ that they are unprovided even with the common virtues which in the very pagans were instilled either by natural reason, experience in living, or the precepts of philosophers.

Unteachable, intractable, quarrelsome, greedy for sensual

pleasures but queasy at the Word of God, agreeable to no
one, evilly suspicious of everyone else but indulgent of themselves—has it at last come to this, that after the efforts of so
many years you should be as bad as possible and still think
yourself as good as possible? that you are a Jew, serving only
dumb substance, and not a Christian? that you think glory
dwells, not privately in the presence of God, but ostentatiously in the sight of men?[49] If you have been walking in the
spirit, not in the flesh, where is the fruit of the spirit? Where
is love? Where is that joy of mind? that peace for all men?
Where is patience? long-suffering? goodness? kindness?
mildness? faith? modesty? continence? purity?[50] Where is
the resemblance to Christ in your character?

"Oh," you say, "I am not a whoremonger, or a thief or a
blasphemer! I practice what I profess."

But what does this mean except "I am not as other men—
robbers, adulterers—and I fast twice on the Sabbath"? Far,
far better the humble publican seeking mercy than that self-
righteous breed who publicize their own good deeds![51]

Moreover, what have you professed? That you would *not*
do the thing you once vowed, at your baptism, that you
would do—be a Christian, which is to say a spiritual man,
not a Jew who because of the petty customs of men would
disobey the mandates of God? Is not being a Christian the
leading of a spiritual life?

Listen to what Paul says to the Romans: "Therefore those
who are in Christ Jesus, who are not walking in accordance
with the flesh, are not condemned. For the law of the Spirit
of life in Christ Jesus has freed me from the law of sin and
death. The thing that was impossible to the law weakened
by reason of the flesh, God, sending His Son in the likeness
of sinful flesh; and by means of sin, condemned sin in the
flesh so that the righteousness of the law might be realized
in us who walk not according to the flesh but the spirit. For
those who live in accordance with the flesh are wise in
things of the flesh, but those who live by the spirit under-

stand those things which pertain to the spirit. The minding
of the flesh is death, but the minding of the spirit is life and
peace. Since carnal wisdom is inimical to God, it is not amenable to God's law, nor can it be. Furthermore, those who are
in the flesh cannot be pleasing to God."[52]

What could be said more fully or more explicitly? Nevertheless, men adept in excusing their own vices and swift to
carp at someone else's think these words do not refer to them
and that what Paul said about walking according to the flesh
applies only to fornicators and lechers. What he said about
the wisdom of the flesh being an enemy to God, that they
twist into an allusion to those who have studied what they
call secular knowledge. One way or another they are con-
gratulating themselves, for they are not fornicators and they
are spectacularly innocent of all branches of learning. As for
the rest of it, living in the spirit, they idly suppose, means
nothing more than doing what they themselves do.

Now, if these people had been as attentive in studying the
language of Paul as they have been intrepid in denouncing
that of Cicero, they would know that the Apostle indisputably calls "flesh" that which is visible and "spirit" that which
is invisible. And everywhere he teaches that the visible ought
to be governed by the invisible, not the invisible by the
visible. Inverting the order, you accommodate Christ to those
things it would be more fitting to accommodate to Christ.[53]

Do you want evidence that the word "flesh" does not pertain solely to lust or debauchery? Listen to what this same
Apostle—doing what he always does—writes to the Colossians: "Let no one mislead you, willing in humility and the
worship of angels, walking in the things he has not seen,
vainly arrogant in the consciousness of his own flesh and
not holding fast to the Head, namely, Christ, from whom the
whole Body, compact and drawing nourishment through its
interlockings and jointures, burgeons into the plenitude of
God."

And if you think he was not referring to those people who

raise a hue and cry about the spiritual interests of others because they themselves are absorbed in certain corporeal observances, listen to what follows: "Therefore, if you are dead
with Christ to this world's preoccupations, why do you pass
judgment as though you were still living in the world?" And
a little later, in calling us away from these things, he says, "If
you have been resurrected with Christ, seek those things
which are above, where Christ is sitting on the right hand of
God. Be wise in those things which are above, not of this
earth."

Then as he hands down the precepts of the spiritual life,
what does he finally advise? Is it that we employ this or
that ritual? That we be dressed thus or so? That we live on
this or that food? That we mumble so many psalms? Nothing
of the sort. What is it then?

"Mortify those elements of yours which are of this earth,"
he says: "fornication, filthiness, lewdness, evil concupiscence,
and idolatrous greed." And a bit later, this: "Now put aside
all wrath, disdain, and malice." Then a little beneath that, he
says, "Freeing yourself of the Old Man with his deeds and
putting on the new man, the one renewed in the knowledge
of God, who created him according to His image."

Who is this "Old Man"? Unquestionably that Adam, of the
earth earthly, whose natural link is with earth, not heaven.
Understand that "earth" here is whatever is visible, and
therefore temporal. Who is the "new" man? Obviously the
celestial Man, descended from heaven; and understand that
"heaven" refers to what is invisible and, accordingly, eternal.

Finally, so that we will not imitate the Jews in trying to
ingratiate ourselves with God by means of certain rituals,
as if there were some magic in ceremonies, he teaches us that
our works are pleasing to God only to the extent that they
are consonant with charity and have originated in charity.
"Above all these things," he says, "hold fast to love, which is
the bond of perfection, and let the peace of Christ the Lord,

in which you have been called members in one Body, triumph in your hearts."[54]

I will give you a plainer example. When Paul is writing to the Galatians he often speaks of both the flesh and the spirit, and he tries to call these people away, not just from bodily lust to chastity, but from Judaism and from their reliance upon forms, into which they had been drawn by false apostles. So, as he reviews here the works of the flesh, note what vices he names: "Manifest are the works of the flesh—fornication, foulness, shamelessness, excess, worship of idols, sorcery, enmity, quarrelsomeness, envy, wrath, brawling, strife, schisms, ill will, murder, drunkenness, carousing, and their like." A little later he says "If we live in the spirit, let us walk in the spirit." Then, as if he were describing a kind of disease that threatens the spirit, he adds this: "Let us not be made eager for empty glory, by turns contentious and envious."[55]

A tree is known by its fruits.[56] I am not impressed by the fact that you never omit a watch, a fast, a period of silence, a prayer, or the rest of the observances of this sort. I will not believe that you are spiritual unless I see the fruits of the spirit. Why should I not insist that these things are carnal when I still detect in you the works of the flesh after you have spent almost a lifetime in the exercise of such formalities, when I find envy worse than a woman's, irascibility and bellicose fierceness, an insatiable lust for wrangling, rabid slander, the viperous poison of the traducing tongue, the haughty spirit, the stiff neck, dubious honesty, vanity, falsehood, flattery?

You judge your brother by what he eats or drinks or by the way he dresses, but Paul judges you by your deeds. Are you any different from carnal worldlings merely because you busy yourself in comparatively trivial demonstrations of the same vices? Which man is worse, the one who succumbs to wrath or enmity or jealousy because he has had a legacy stolen from him, a daughter violated, a relative injured, be-

cause he wants to obtain some office or favor from a prince
—or you who do things much worse, I am ashamed to say,
for no reason at all? The more trivial the occasion for sin, the
greater, not the less, the blame. The seriousness of the occasion is not significant, only that you have yielded to the same
passion. Or, rather, it signifies to this extent: the more hardened a person is, the slighter the occasion it takes to entice
him from honorable behavior.

I am not speaking now of these monks whose habits even
the world abominates, but of people whom the mass of men
gape at as if they were not human but angelic. Still, even
these people need not be offended by my words, which note
the vices, not the persons. If they are good men, though, let
them even be glad if anyone admonishes them in those matters which are essential to spiritual health. Nor am I unaware that many of them, supported by learning and character, have tasted the mysteries of the spirit. But, as Livy
says, it usually happens that numbers prevail over quality.[57]
And even so, if we may speak frankly, do we not see the most
exacting type of monks putting their chief emphasis in worship either upon ceremonies or upon a certain mode of
psalmody or upon certain physical tasks? If one were to
examine them closely and look into their spiritual condition,
he would find very few who are not walking in the flesh.

Here is the source of great inconstancy of spirit—now
shaking with fear when there is no reason for fear, at another
time being sluggishly negligent when the peril is greatest.
Here also is the cause of that—to put it gently—perpetual infancy in Christ, so that with inverted standards of worth
most of us do the things which in themselves amount to
nothing and neglect those which are alone essential. We pass
our entire lives under tutors, always subject to supervision
and without ever aspiring to liberty of spirit or to growing
up in the fullness of charity.

"Stand firm," cries Paul to the Galatians, "and do not be

tied again to the yoke of servitude."[58] In another place he says, "So our schoolmaster has been the law in Christ, so that we may be justified by faith; but when faith comes, we are no longer under a schoolmaster. For you are all sons of God by faith, which is in Christ Jesus."[59] And a bit later: "Even so, when we were little children we were subject to the principles of the world. But when the right time came, God sent His Son, made of woman and made under the law, that He might redeem those under the law and that we might be adopted as His sons. Since you are the sons of God, then, God sent the spirit of His Son into your hearts, crying, 'Abba, Father!' Therefore he is no longer a servant, but a son."[60] And elsewhere again, "For you have been called into freedom as brothers," he says: "only let yourselves not turn your liberty into a convenience of the flesh, but serve one another in the love of the spirit. For all the law is fulfilled in one injunction: that you love your neighbor as yourself. But if you bite and prey upon one another, look out that you are not mutually devoured."[61] Again, he writes this to the Romans: "For you have not received the spirit of adoption as sons of God, in which we cry 'Abba, Father.' "[62] And he makes the same point when he writes to Timothy: "Train yourself," he says, "to goodness, for bodily exercise is useful only for trifling things but righteousness is useful in all things."[63] And to the Corinthians: "The Lord is that Spirit. Where the Spirit is, there is liberty also."[64]

But why mention one or two such passages? Paul is engrossed in this point, that we should spurn the strife-ridden flesh and be firm in the spirit, the begetter of love and liberty. On the one hand, the flesh, bondage, unrest, contention are inseparable companions; on the other, the spirit, peace, love, freedom. This is what the Apostle teaches everywhere. Do we need a better instructor in religion, especially when all of the Holy Scripture agrees with him? This was the most important commandment in Mosaic law; this Christ reiterates and makes perfect in the Gospels. For this purpose, especially, was He born; and He died in order that He might teach us, not to imitate the Jews, but to love.

After that last supper, how anxiously, how tenderly He instructed His disciples, not in what they should eat or drink, but in the love they should keep for one another.[65] What else does He teach, indeed, what else does John, the fellow priest of Paul, seek except that we love one another? And although Paul commends charity everywhere, as I have said, when he writes to the Corinthians he values it even before miracles and prophecy and the tongues of angels.[66]

And do not tell me, presently, that charity consists of frequent church attendance or genuflecting in front of the images of saints or burning candles or repeating a specified number of little prayers. God is not impressed by such routines. Paul calls it love to raise up one's neighbor, to consider all men as members of the same Body, to think of us all as being one in Christ, to rejoice in the Lord because of your brother's good fortune as much as your own, to remedy his misfortunes as if they were your own. Admonish him gently when he errs, teach the benighted, lift up the fallen, console the downcast, aid the person in difficulties, assist those in need, and devote all your wealth, zeal, and effort to this one end above everything else: serving, in Christ, as many people as you possibly can. Just as He was neither born for Himself, nor lived for Himself nor died for Himself, so we should be devoted to the welfare of others, not to our own.

If this were to happen, nothing would be happier or more gracious than the lives of the professionally religious, whereas now we see them, quite to the contrary, harsh, gloomy, and full of Judaic superstition, free from none of the vices of the laity and in some cases even worse. If Augustine, whom many brag of as the founder of this kind of life, were to come back to earth, he surely would not even know such men and would roundly declare that he himself would have cared for nothing less than this mode of existence; that he had instituted a method of living, not according to the anxious credulity of the Jews, but the rule of the Apostles.

But even now I hear how some people will answer me, and with some reason: "One must be scrupulous in very minor observances," they will say, "lest one gradually slide into graver sins. "

I hear them, and I agree. You should be much more careful, however, not to cling so hard to the least important that you entirely forget the most important. In the first case the danger is more apparent, but in this other, more grave. Escape Scylla in such a way that you do not fall into Charybdis. Observing such rituals as those is all very well, but relying upon them is perilous. Paul does not forbid your using the physical elements, but he wants the person who is free in Christ not to be subservient to these ceremonies. He does not condemn the law requiring certain corporeal rites if one applies it properly. Perhaps you will not be a good man without these things, but they do not make you good. They will be conducive to piety only if you employ them for that purpose; if you begin to revel in them, they immediately extinguish all that piety. The Apostle set no store by the deeds of Abraham, which everyone knows were unexceptionable. Do you, then, have confidence in your own? God turns His back upon the sacrificial victims and Sabbaths and new-moon holy days of His people, all of which He himself had created. Will you, then, dare to match your petty observances against the precepts of divine law?

Listen to God, made sick and angry by such stuff: "What do I care about a flock of your sacrificial victims? I am sated with them. I don't want the slaughter of rams, the greasy fat and blood of bull calves and lambs and he goats. When you come into My presence, who has asked for these things from your hands so that you might walk in My dwelling place? Offer Me no more useless sacrifices; the burning is an

abomination to Me. I will not stomach your new moon, your
Sabbath, and the rest of your ceremonies. Your gatherings
are iniquitous; My soul loathes your first days and your
solemn rituals. These performances oppress Me; I have with
difficulty endured them. And when you stretch out your
hands to Me, I will turn My eyes from you. When you multiply your prayers, I will not listen to you."[67]

Now, when God refers to the observances and rituals of
the sacraments, as well as to the multiplication of prayers, is
He not pointing out with His finger, so to speak, those who
measure their religion by the number of psalms or prayers?
And note also how the prophet eloquently underlines God's
distaste and the fact that He now could endure neither seeing these things nor listening to them. What things, pray?
Unquestionably those rites which He himself had handed
down to be preserved so devoutly, and which had been so
meticulously preserved for so many years by holy kings and
prophets. But these things He nevertheless detests because
they belong to carnal law. But are you confident that your
little home-made ceremonies are relevant to spiritual law?

Similarly, in another place He orders the same prophet to
cry out incessantly and to raise his voice like a trumpet, in a
way fitting for a matter of serious import and one worthy of
stringent censure, such a matter as could scarcely be
broached to such men without much ado.

"They seek Me," He says, "from day to day and wish to
know My ways, like a nation which has done justice and
which has not abandoned the judgment of their God. They
ask Me for the decisions of justice and wish to come near
to God. 'Why have we fasted," they cry, "and You have not
considered us? We have abased our hearts, and You have
not known us.' But look; on the very day you fast your own
will comes to the fore, and you hunt up again all the people
who owe you money. You fast for strife and debate and to
strike wickedly with your fist. Do not fast, as you always

have up to the present time, so that your uproar may re-sound to high heaven. Is this the kind of fasting I have elected, that a man should vex his soul for the length of a day? That he should bow himself into the shape of a hoop and cover his head with sackcloth and ashes? Will you call that fasting, or a day pleasing to the Lord?"[68]

Now what shall we say of this? Is God condemning what He himself commanded? No. What, then? Only our remain-ing in the flesh of the law and putting our trust in something of no account, this is really what He condemns.

Therefore, he shows in each instance what He would have approved. "You must be cleansed of the world," He says; "you must remove the evil of your thoughts from My sight."[69] When you hear the phrase "evil of your thoughts," does He not plainly refer to the spirit and the inward man? The eyes of God look, not at palpable things but at the hidden; neither does He judge according to what the eyes see nor rebuke according to what the ears hear.[70] The foolish vir-gins, who were outwardly comely but inwardly empty, He did not acknowledge.[71] He did not know those who, with their lips, say "Lord, Lord."[72]

Finally, He warns that the practice of a spiritual life con-sists not so much in ritualism as in the love of one's fellow men. Seek judgment, give help to the oppressed, defend the orphan, protect the widow[73]—such injunctions as these had He appended to that other place where He was talking about fasting. "Is not this," He says, "a more important fasting that I have chosen: that you strike off the bonds of wickedness, remove the burdens weighing men down, free those who have been buffeted and relieve every oppression? that you break your bread with the hungry and take the needy and dispossessed into your home? that when you see a man naked, you cover him, and that you not scorn your own flesh?"[74]

Very well, what should a Christian do? Neglect the man-

dates of the Church? Scorn the honorable traditions of his
ancestors? Censure all pious customs?

No, in reality if he is weak he will observe them as things
necessary, but if he is strong and mature he will observe
them much more assiduously, lest his own knowledge be detrimental to his weaker brother and destroy a person for
whom Christ died.[75] One need not abandon these things,
but one must observe other things as well. Palpable observances are not condemned, but the impalpable take precedence. Visible forms of worship are not condemned, but God
is not pleased by anything but the invisible state of righteousness. God is a spirit, and He is moved by spiritual
sacrifices.[76]

It is shameful for Christians not to know what even a certain pagan poet knew who, in treating of *pietas,* says this:

> If God is spirit, as poetic lays declare,
> A mind kept pure is an offering most fair.[77]

Nor should we look down on the author, even if he was a
pagan or a minor figure; the remark is worthy of a great divine and, as I have plainly observed, has been understood by
as few men as it has been read by many. It means that like
is attracted to like. You suppose God is best influenced by
a slaughtered bull or the smoke of incense, as if He were
flesh and blood, but He is Mind, and of the purest, most
quintessential form. Accordingly, He must be worshipped
in the best sense by unadulterated mind and spirit.

You think a lighted candle is a sacrifice, but David says
a contrite and sorrowful spirit is the sacrifice to make to
God,[78] and though He has disparaged the blood of he goats
or of bull calves, He will not disparage an humble and re-
pentant heart. If you do the things discernible to the eyes
of men, you should be even more careful to do what is of
interest to the eyes of God.[79] What difference does it make
if the body is decked out in a cowl of sanctity when the

heart wears the garments of worldliness? If the outer man is wrapped in a fresh white robe, then the vestments of the inner man should also be white as snow. If you preserve periods of silence away from home, see to it much more devoutly that the mind is inwardly serene. You go through your genuflections in the visible church; they achieve nothing if in the temple of your heart you stand erect to confront God. You venerate the wood of the Cross; more importantly, attend to the mystery of that Cross.

Do you keep fasting days and refrain from eating even those things which do a man no harm, but at the same time fail to give up bawdy talk, which does harm both to your own moral sense and someone else's? Does your body go without food while your soul gorges itself upon husks fit for pigs? So you ornament a sanctuary made of stone and you venerate holy places? Of what use is that if the sanctuary of your heart, whose wall Ezekiel pierced,[80] is profaned by the abominations of Egypt? Outwardly you observe the Sabbath, but inwardly everything is strident with the bedlam of vice. Your body commits no adultery, but you are covetous; actually, your mind is an adulterer. Vocally you chant and sing, but you should listen within to what your heart is saying; with your lips you utter benedictions but with your heart, curses. In body you confine yourself to a narrow cell, but in your thoughts you wander the whole earth. You listen physically to the Word of God, but you ought to hear it spiritually.

What does the prophet say? That unless you have listened inwardly your soul will cry out.[81] And what do you read in the Gospel? That those who see may not see, and those who hear may not hear.[82] And again the prophet says, "You will listen with the ear and you will not understand."[83] Happy, therefore, are those who inwardly hear the Word of God. Happy are those to whom the Lord speaks in this way, and their souls will be made whole. This is the ear David orders that daughter of the king to incline, she whose glory, like needlework of gold, is wholly inward.[84]

Finally, what does it signify that you do not commit sins which in your heart you lust for? What does it signify that in the market place you do good deeds which are totally unlike what goes on inside you? Is it so very important that you make a physical trip to Jerusalem, when in your own heart there is a veritable Sodom, an Egypt, a Babylon? It is no great thing to have planted your earthly shoes in the footsteps of Christ, but it is of gravest importance to follow Him in your affections. If it is so important to have touched the tomb of the Lord, will it not be more important to have expressed in your life the holy mystery of his burial? You confess your sins before a mortal priest; see to it how you confess before God, for to confess before Him is to be inwardly penitent. Perhaps you believe your sins are removed once and for all by a wax seal, by giving a little money or by making a little pilgrimage. You are completely off the track. The wound has been inflicted within, and the remedy must be applied there. Your will has been corrupted: you have loved what deserved to be hated and hated what deserved to be loved. Sweet has been bitter to you; and bitter, sweet.

I am not impressed by your public performances, but if you change and will instead begin to hate, avoid, and scorn what in wrongdoing you used to love, if the thing that once smacked of gall now tastes sweet to your spiritual palate, then I am finally getting the evidence of sound health. Magdalene loved deeply, and many sins were forgiven her.[85] The more you love Christ, the more you will hate your sins, for hatred of sin accompanies love of virtue as a shadow accompanies the body. I would rather that you loathe, inwardly and genuinely, your bad habits than that you deprecate them verbally over and over again before a priest.

Therefore, as we have been pointing out, with reference to certain examples in the whole theater of this visible world—

in ancient law and in new, in every injunction of the Church, and finally in you yourself and in all human affairs—the form constitutes a kind of flesh; the inner content, the spirit. If we are not to turn these values upside down, nor put so much confidence in what is palpable except to the degree that it contributes to the improvement of what is essential, we must look always to the spirit and to those things which reflect love. Then we shall not become lugubrious and feeble, as these men are; always children, as the proverb has it; dry bones, to quote the prophet;[86] spiritless, sluggish, dull, quarrelsome, spiteful, muttering. Rather, we shall be triumphant in Christ, filled with charity, strong and ready for any eventuality, indifferent to trifles, aspiring toward excellence, full of eagerness and wisdom.

Whoever rejects this wisdom, him the Lord of all wisdom also rejects; for ignorance, which normally goes along with an incapacity for learning, and she whom the Greeks neatly call Philautia, cause us—as Isaiah says—to put our trust in bagatelles and to talk of vanities;[87] to conceive mischief and bring forth iniquity;[88] to become fearful and abject slaves to Judaic ceremony.

Paul is referring to this sort of people when he says, "I bear witness that they have the zeal of God, but not in accordance with knowledge."[89] What was it they did not know? Surely the fact that Christ is the ultimate mark of the law, and that Christ is, moreover, Spirit and Love.

Isaiah describes more plainly the unhappy and futile slavery to the flesh on the part of these men: "Therefore, my people have been led off in captivity because they did not have wisdom. And their leaders have perished of hunger, and a multitude of them have died of thirst."[90]

It is not strange that the people, the untutored masses, serve the principles of this world and know nothing except what they are told. It is more remarkable, though, that the Princes, so to speak, of the Christian religion are withering

and parching, perishing of hunger and thirst in this same
captivity. Why of hunger? Because they have not learned
from Christ to break the loaves of barley.[91] They lick at only
the dry husks; they do not dig out the kernel. And why of
thirst? Because they have not learned from Moses to strike
water from the rock of the Spirit,[92] nor do they drink from
the streams of the living Waters which flow from the womb
of Christ.[93] This surely was said of the spirit, not of the flesh.

Therefore, my Brother, in order that you may not, even
with exacerbating labors, have such heavy going, but may
instead with moderate exercise develop maturity and vigor
in Christ, be scrupulous in following this rule: do not wish
to crawl on the ground with filthy beasts but, ever relying
upon those wings which Plato thinks are engendered in souls
by the fervor of love,[94] steadily aspire to mount—as if by
certain steps of Jacob's ladder[95]—from body to spirit, from
the visible world to the invisible, from the letter to the es-
sence, from the sensible to the intelligible, from multiplicity
to oneness. Thus the Lord will in His turn draw near to whoever draws near to Him;[96] and if you will try with all your
might to rise out of the darkness and confusion of your sen-
sory experience, He will graciously come to meet you from
His inaccessible Light and inscrutable Stillness,[97] where not
only every agitation of sensuality but every shadowy phan-
tom of powers intelligible is put to rest.

FIFTEEN

The Sixth Rule

(Do Not Follow Popular Opinion but Only Christ)

AND, SINCE IN extempore writing one thing suggests another,
I am going to work in a sixth rule, derived in some degree
from the preceding, and as essential to the moral health of

everyone as it is a matter of concern to few. This rule is that
the mind of a man eager for Christ should part company as
sharply as possible both with the actions and the opinions
of the general run of people, and not look for an example of
virtue from any quarter other than Christ alone. He is the
sole Archetype; whoever departs from Him by the width of
a finger departs from rectitude and is missing the way.

Similarly, in his *Republic* Plato makes a strong case, as he
often does, against the possibility that anyone who does not
saturate his mind with definite concepts of right and wrong
can consistently maintain virtue.[1] But how much more dangerous it is when fallacious notions of these matters which
pertain to spiritual well-being deeply infiltrate the mind! He
thinks this, therefore, is of prime importance: that his guar-
dians, who must be free from every vice, engrave upon their
minds—and as indelibly as the most sacred laws—the soundest precepts as to what ought to be cultivated and what
avoided. For everyone expresses in his character the deepest
and most persuasive convictions of his mind.

To that end Christians ought to take special pains that
children, even from infancy, imbibe at the hands of learned
teachers convictions worthy of Christ along with the caress-
ing of their nurses and the kisses of their parents, for nothing
sinks more deeply into the mind, or clings more tenaciously,
than that which is taught, as Fabius says, in tender years.[2]
Keep far away from the little ears of babes the amatory dit-
ties which Christians sing at home and everywhere else, songs
filthier than the average pagan ever tolerated. Let them not
hear their mother wailing about some piece of property's being damaged, or crying her eyes out because she has been left
desolate and wretched by the loss of a sister. Let them not
hear their father charging with cowardice someone who did
not pay back an injury with interest and lavishly praising
those who have piled up the most property, no matter how.

Prone to vice, human nature catches immediately upon an

evil model as naphtha upon a nearby fire. At every age, however, all these vulgar errors ought to be plucked out by the
very roots and wholesome precepts implanted in their stead
to grow so strong that nothing can uproot them. One who
has done this will pursue virtue voluntarily and without
difficulty, and will deem those who do otherwise as deserving of pity, not emulation.

This is the point of that remark of Socrates—not a foolish
one, in spite of Aristotle's criticism—that virtue is nothing
but the knowledge of what to avoid and what to cultivate.[3]
Not that Socrates had failed to see the distinction between
awareness of the good and the love of it, but just as Demosthenes asserts that pronunciation is the first, second, and
third principle of oratory[4]—signifying, of course, a role so
special that he considers the whole are included in it—just so
does Socrates, disagreeing with Protagoras, argue convincingly that knowledge contributes so much to every virtue of importance that vices spring up in no other way than
from false beliefs. For surely both the man who loves Christ
and the man who loves pleasure, money, and empty honors
are following what is for them the sweet, the good, the beautiful. The one, however, is deluded by ignorance, seizing
upon things acridly bitter instead of sweetness, eschewing
what is sweetest in place of the bitter, pursuing unadulterated poison instead of the good and profitable, fearing as
loss what is really gain, judging beautiful what is really foul,
feeling he ought to be ashamed of the one thing that is
truly excellent.

Furthermore, if one has been deeply persuaded, and if he
has fed and nourished the tissue of his mind with the idea
that only goodness is excellent, most delightful, most fair,
most honorable, most useful; that on the other hand only
baseness is an evil thing, a torment, a filthiness, something
damnable and shameful; and if he judges these matters not
by mass opinion but by their intrinsic nature, it is impossible

that, assuming steadfastness in his persuasion, he should cling very long to his vices. The mob has long been the worst authority, not only for conduct but for understanding, nor were human affairs ever so well managed that the worst things did not please the most people.

Guard yourself against this kind of thinking: "Everyone does this. In these footsteps my elders have trod; of this opinion is such-and-such great philosopher, such-and-such eminent divine. This is the way important people live. This is the practice of royalty; this is the way the most important bishops and pontiffs regularly behave. Surely these people are not a part of the mob."

But do not let imposing names sway you. I judge the mob, not by eminence, but by what is in the heart. The mob consists of those people in Plato's Cave who, at the mercy of their passions, value the empty appearances of Things rather than Realities.[5] Is a man not acting preposterously who tries to measure, not the stone by the ruler, but the ruler by the stone? But is he not much more foolish who strives to adapt, not the behavior of men to Christ, but Christ to the behavior of men? Do not believe, then, that something is right because important people or because the majority practice it, but that it is right if it tallies with the principles of Christ.

As a matter of fact, whatever is pleasing to most people you should, for his very reason, eye with suspicion. Small is the number, as it will always be, of those who cherish Christian simplicity, humility, and truth. Small but blessed, since only to that number is the Kingdom of Heaven due.[6] The path of virtue is narrow, and very few travel it; but no other path leads to life.[7] What kind of model does a wise builder examine—the routine practice or the best? Painters, too, study only the best pictures. Now, our example is Christ, who alone embodies every principle of living happily; Him we may emulate without qualification. As for men of rectitude, we can appropriately use one or another as a model only to the extent that he corresponds to the archetypal goodness of Christ. Where the mass of Christians are concerned, however, consider that as far as ethical principles are concerned no one has ever been more corrupt, even among pagans.

Touching upon their faith, moreover, let them make sure what they believe in. Unquestionably, faith without the character consonant with faith comes to so little that it may even lead to a mountain of damnation.[8] Study the history of the ancients and compare them with the morality of these times. When was uprightness ever so little esteemed? When was wealth, acquired no matter how, ever more highly regarded? What age did these lines of Horace ever fit more neatly?

By the unfailing grace of Her Majesty, Money,
A well-to-do wife comes equipped with honor and friends,
Not to mention beauty and patrician family.[9]

Or another remark of the same poet?

For without property,
Lineage and virtue are more useless than seaweed.[10]

Does anyone nowadays not take this ironic mockery at face value?

O citizens, citizens! Get money first!
Virtue after hard cash![11]

When was debauchery ever more rampant? When have lust and fornication been more brazen or less punished or in better repute? This is a time when princes are indulgent toward their own vices discovered in other people and when everyone thinks it splendid to sin after the manner of courtiers. Who does not consider poverty the worst of evils and disgrace? The time once was when harsh taunts were hurled from the stage at lechers, misers, the insolent, the greedy. In the shows of pagans the common people cheered when vices were censured—the same vices which today our leading Christians applaud when they see them villainously extolled. The play-goers of Athens would hardly stand for an actor's declaiming, from one of the tragedies of Euripides, the words of a certain miser who gave precedence to money over all other goods of human life; and clearly they would have hissed and thrown out the actor along with the whole play had not the author quickly got up and directed them to wait a little while and see what happened to that money-lover.[12]

How many examples there are among pagans of men who from their sound management of public affairs brought nothing back to their modest household but an honorable reputation, who held fidelity more important than wealth, virtue dearer than life, who could neither be puffed up by good fortune nor broken by adversity, who preferred honorable risks to pleasures and, satisfied only by the consciousness of a good life, sought neither honor nor riches nor any other advantages of fortune. And I need not mention the integrity of Phocion, the poverty—more potent than riches—of Fabricius, the magnanimity of Camillus, the moral strictness of Brutus, the purity of Pythagoras, the invincible temperance of Socrates, the uprightness of Cato, and a thousand fine examples of all the virtues which we read of everywhere —to our great shame, indeed—in the annals of the Spartans, the Persians, the Athenians, the Romans.

As he himself testifies in the records of his own *Confessions*, the saintly Aurelius Augustine, long before he became a Christian, despised money, held worldly honors in contempt, was indifferent to glory, and put such a constant check upon voluptuousness that as a young man he was content with one woman, to whom he gave all the loyalty of marriage.[13]

One rarely finds such spirits, such examples among our courtiers and churchmen—or, let me add, among our monks! Or if someone of this sort should appear in these quarters, he would be like an ass among apes,[14] a show piece and a joke; he would be unanimously dismissed as silly, doltish, hypocritical, ignorant of the world, a victim of melancholy, mad, less than a man!

Thus we Christians do homage to the teaching of Christ, thus we express it—so that nowadays nothing is popularly considered more foolish, more despicable, more humiliating than to be a Christian heart and soul. As if Christ either dwelled on earth to no purpose, or Christianity is something different now from what it used to be, or does not apply to everyone in the same fashion.

From these people, then, I would have you differ radically and weigh all values solely in terms of the fellowship of Christ. Is there anyone anywhere who does not think it a fine thing and one of the rarest advantages to be born of distinguished stock, what they call the nobility? Do not let yourself be impressed when you hear the knowing people of this world, grave men invested with the weightiest authority, debating very earnestly and with wrinkled brows, as if it were something that mattered, the various gradations of pedigree and with great to-do spouting off portentous prittle-prattle, or when you see others so arrogant at the thought of their grandfathers and great-great-grandfathers that they judge the rest of mankind, compared to them, to be scarcely human.

On the contrary, like Democritus you should laugh at the folly of these people and consider—as is really the case—that the highest, indeed the only, nobility is to be reborn in Christ, to be grafted upon His Body and become one spirit with God.[15] Let others be the sons of kings; for you, let it be of supreme importance that you are called, and actually are, the child of God. Let other men congratulate themselves on being busy in the courts of princes; as for you, prefer like David to be humble in the house of the Lord.[16] Keep in mind those people Christ loved: the helpless, the "fools," the lowly, in terms of this world.[17] In Adam we are all born without rank; in Christ we are all one. The real nobility is to despise false nobility; the real nobility is to be a servant of Christ. Consider as your ancestors those whose virtues you emulate.

Listen to what the best assessor of nobility has said in the Gospel about the Jews who were preening themselves over Abraham's being the founder of their race. And what kind of a founder, indeed? Not only illustrious and powerful, the conqueror of kings, but commended by God Himself for his holy virtue. Who would not consider this a marked distinction, a sufficient reason for boasting? But listen to what they heard! "You have been fathered by Satan, and you do the work of your father."[18]

And hear Paul applying the rule of the Master to this question of lineage: "Not all who are of Israel in the matter of circumcision," he says, "are Israelites, nor are all the seed of Abraham his children."[19]

The shameful baseness is to serve immorality, to have no kinship with Christ, who acknowledges no one failing to do the will of His Father in heaven.[20] The truly base-born bastard is he who has the Devil as his father, and whoever does the Devil's works has him as father, unless Christ has lied to us.[21] But Truth does not know how to lie. The highest degree of gentility, then, is to be son and heir of God, brother and co-heir of Christ. As for the marks of distinction of those other people, let them look for whatever they wish. The badges of Christians, true, are common to all men, but most honorable: the cross, the crown of thorns, the nails, the spear —the Master's insignia that Paul rejoiced to wear on his own body.[22]

So you see how differently from the way most people do I would have you feel about noble breeding. Who among the general run of men does not call a person happy, rich, and blessed if he has a lot of money piled up in his home? But you should deem happy enough—really the only genuinely happy man—the one who has Christ, the supreme Good; who has purchased that precious pearl of a pure mind either at the cost of everything else or of his body itself;[23] who has found the treasure of a wisdom more valuable than all riches;[24] who from a most bountiful Christ has acquired the gold tempered and tested for making him truly wealthy.[25]

What, then, are those baubles the crowd prizes—gold, gems, real estate? Misnamed riches, actually briars which according to the parable of the Gospel choke out the seeds of the Holy Word.[26] Baggage, weighted down by which, men cannot follow an unencumbered Christ over a narrow path or enter the low door into the Kingdom of Heaven. If you have more money than Midas or Croesus, do not imagine yourself better for it even by a hair, but rather the more fettered, the more burdened, the more impeded. The man who can firmly reject such things is sufficiently well off; the man to whom Christ has promised that nothing will be lacking has enough to look forward to. Anyone who has savored the manna of the Holy Word will not hunger; anyone who has put on Christ will not be naked.[27] Think of a person as damned only to the extent that he has deviated from real goodness and grown in viciousness. Think of true wealth as the improvement of the mind through the increase of virtue. Think that you lack nothing if you have Him in whom everything else is incorporated.

But what is this thing the wretched call pleasure? Surely nothing less than what it is called. What is that then? Unadulterated madness and—as the Greeks put it—the laughter of Ajax,[28] an alluring poison, a delightful ruin. The one and only real pleasure is the joy of a sound conscience; the most sumptuous feasts are the study of the Holy Scriptures; the most delightful songs, the psalms of the Holy Spirit; the most festive society, the communion of all the saints; the keenest delights, the enjoyment of truth. Only cleanse your eyes, your ears, your palate, and Christ will begin to be sweet to you. Once He has been truly savored, even if Milesians,[29] sybarites, libertines, Epicureans—in brief, all the contrivers of voluptuousness—should gather all their pleasures together, they would all seem disgusting in comparison with His.

A thing tasted is not durably pleasant unless it is tasty to a healthy state. If water tastes like wine to someone with a fever, one does not call that pleasure but disease. You are deceived if you do not believe that tears are far more gratifying to the devout than ribald jokes and horseplay to the impious; that fasting is not more pleasant to the one than their heathcocks, pheasants, partridges, sturgeon or flatfish are to the others; that the frugal little tables set with Pythagorean cabbages and beans are not more sumptuous by far than the finical luxuriousness of such people as they.[30]

True pleasure, then, is to be lured, not by spurious delights, but by the love of Christ. Note how the world perverts even the terms *love* and *hate*. When a youth is madly enamored of a girl, this condition most people call love, though nothing is more truly hatred. Real love desires to bring about the good of others, even at its own expense; but what does he have in mind but his own pleasure? He loves himself, not her; as a matter of fact, he really does not love even himself, for no one can love another unless he first loves himself, and in the right way. And no one can hate another person unless he first hates himself.

Nevertheless, to love well is sometimes to hate well, and to hate deeply is to love deeply. Therefore, any man who for some slight pleasure (as he imagines it to be) sets traps for a girl with blandishments and presents in order to rob her of the most precious thing she has, her honor and chastity, her innocence, her purity of mind, her reputation—does he seem to you to be loving or hating? Surely no hatred could be more brutal than this! Or when foolish parents indulge the faults of their children, is it not commonly remarked how tenderly these people love their offspring? But the truth is, how cruelly they hate them, who while they accommodate their policy to their emotions are negligent of their children's moral health. What else does that most malicious Foe, the Devil, want from us than that by sinning here with impunity we may incur everlasting punishment?

People call a prince a mild and gentle master if he winks at certain crimes, or even favors them, so that the more lurid their sins are, the more immune they are to punishment. But through His prophet what else does the Lord threaten for those people He considers unworthy of His mercy?

"And I shall not punish your daughters when they fornicate," He says, "and your daughters-in-law when they commit adultery."[31] What did He promise David? "I will visit their iniquities with the scourge and their sins with whipping. Nevertheless, I will not take my mercy from him."[32]

You see that in Christ all things are changed and their names are reversed. Anyone who loves himself in the wrong way ruinously hates himself. Anyone who is wrongly indulgent toward himself is cruelly tyrannical. To care properly is to be neglectful; to hurt rightly is to do good. To squander rightly is to save. You will be caring best for yourself if you despise your fleshly desires. If you are hard enough on the vices, you will do the man a favor; if you destroy the sinner, you will have saved the man. If you obliterate what man has made, you will preserve what God has made.

Going further, what does popular error consider strength and weakness, courage and cowardice? Does it not call strong the man who can easily injure anyone he wants to? Even though being able to do harm is a hateful power, this is what strength means to those people: the ability to cause injury, something common to the Spanish fly, the scorpion, and the Devil himself. But only God is truly powerful, and He is not able to do harm even if He wished and would not wish it if He could, since it is His nature to do good.

How, then, does this mighty fellow harm a man? Will he steal his money? Beat him? Take his life? If he does this to a good man he has done him a good turn rather than an injury;

if, however, he does it to a wicked man, he has provided the occasion for evil, to be sure, but he has harmed only himself, for no one is harmed by anyone except himself.[33] Nobody gets ready to hurt someone else unless he has already hurt himself far more deeply. If you are prepared to steal my money, you have already inflicted the gravest injury upon yourself because you have lost the feeling of charity. You cannot give me a wound until you have first received one much worse. You cannot murder my body until you first murder your own soul. But does not Paul, who was most valiant in enduring evil and most incapable of inflicting it, rejoice that in Christ he was able to do all things?[34]

The crowd calls brave and spirited the man who fiercely and uncontrollably boils with fury at any trivial offense whatsoever and pays back hurt for hurt, insult for insult. On the other hand, anyone who stomachs an injury he has received, and passes over it, him they call a pitiful, spiritless, good-for-nothing coward. In point of fact, however, what is more alien to greatness of mind than to let one's equanimity be affected by a mere word and to be so incapable of despising another's folly that you don't consider yourself a man unless you return evil for evil? How much more courageous to be able to disregard any injury, and with a lofty and generous spirit, moreover, pay back good for bad.

I would not call the man brave who is daring against the enemy, who mounts the wall and, holding life cheap, exposes his head to every peril—a quality he shares with almost any professional swordsman. But the man who can conquer his own mind, who from his heart can wish good for those who wish him evil, can deserve well of those who deserve ill, can pray for those who curse him—that man deserves to be called courageous and of noble spirit.

Let us also look closely at what the world calls glory, ignominy, and shame. Let us say that you are praised. For what reason? By whom?

If it is for odious reasons and by odious people, that kind

of honor is spurious, actually a rebuke. Suppose you are disparaged, jeered at. Why? And by whom? If it is on account
of your virtue, your integrity, then assuredly it is by bad men,
and that kind of ridicule is no shame. Indeed there is no
sounder commendation. Let the whole world hoot and hiss
at you: nothing can be inglorious if Christ approves it, and
regardless of what makes mortal men applaud and cry
"bravo, bravo!," it can be nothing but shameful if it is dis-
pleasing to God.

People everywhere call it wisdom to work hard for
property, to keep a close grip on what you get and to provide
for the distant future. Thus we hear men everywhere say
earnestly, "He is a frugal man, a judicious, knowing, far-
sighted man" about someone who gets impressively rich in a
short time. And this is the world—itself a liar and like its
father.[35] But what does Truth say? "Fool, tonight I will require your soul of you."[36]

He had filled his barns with harvest, he had stuffed all his
storehouses with provisions, he had saved up a great deal of
money at home. He thought everything had been provided
for, not that after the manner of wild beasts he might gloat
over his heaped up riches like a threadbare custodian, as
poets tell us the dragon guarded the golden fleece,[37] but that
he might enjoy his possessions. Nevertheless, the Gospel calls
this man a fool. For what is greater madness than to lose the
real thing by gaping at illusions, a performance we are in
the habit of laughing at in the well-known dog of Aesop's
fable? And in the behavior of Christians is it not more laughable? Or, rather, more a matter for tears?

Look at him as you would the inept business man, one who
does not know the comic poet's remark that:

> Slighting money at the right moment
> is sometimes the way to make it.[38]

and who takes a small gain now because he does not know
that a greater loss will follow. And how much more foolish

to provide with such anxious solicitude for this constantly mutable life of shadows the things God must needs provide anyway, but to take no thought for the life to come, which we must pass in everlasting wretchedness unless we provide for it with the greatest concern.

Or consider another error. People call clever and knowing the fellow who, seizing upon every scrap of idle gossip, is aware of what is going on everywhere: the condition business is in, what the king of Britain is up to, what is new at Rome, what has got under way in France, how the Danes or the Scythians are getting along, what the statesmen have in mind. In short, a man who can prattle about every piece of business of the whole human race—him they call wise.

But what is more thoughtless or naive than to pry into those affairs which are happening far away and are of no concern to you, yet not so much as think of what goes on in your own heart and which concerns you alone? You tell me of troubles in England; tell me instead about the uprisings in your own breast: anger, envy, lust, ambition. To what extent have these rebellious passions been subdued? What are the prospects for victory? How much of this warring element has been dispersed? How has reason been armed? If in these matters you have been vigilant both of eye and ear, if here you have been sagacious and prudent, I will say you are truly wise and that charge which the world is in the habit of hurling at us I will turn back upon itself. The man who knows nothing of himself knows nothing at all.

If you will examine all the concerns, joys, hopes, fears, desires, and beliefs of mortal men by this standard, you will find all of them riddled with error. They call good evil and evil good; they make sweet sour and sour sweet, light darkness and darkness light.[39] And this practice, as a matter of fact, is characteristic of the large majority of men. But you must simultaneously scorn them (lest you want to be like them) and pity them enough to want them to become as you are. One should, in the words of Augustine, both weep for those who deserve mockery and mock those who deserve tears.

"Guard against conforming in evil to this temporal world; be reformed in newness of understanding so that you may approve, not what captivates men, but what is the will of God: the good, the satisfying, the perfect."[40] If you begin to look around at what most other people are doing or to listen to what they are thinking, you are on dangerous ground and clearly slipping. As a son of light and life, let the dead bury their dead; let the blind leaders of blind followers descend into the pit together. Do not let the eyes of your heart stray in any direction from Christ, your Exemplar.

Following the lead of Truth, you will not go astray; walking in His radiance you will not stumble in darkness. With this light shining clearly before you, you will distinguish the false good from the true one, the real evil from the apparent. You will shudder at and not imitate the blindness of the mob who rage more feverishly than any narrow sea after the empty mockery of material things and experience every vicissitude of passion: anger, envy, love, hate, hope, fear, joy, grief. Brahmans, cynics, and stoics are accustomed to doggedly upholding their own teachings; and even with the whole world protesting and everyone hooting and hissing at them, they nevertheless stubbornly stick to what they have once come to believe. Have the courage to fix deeply in your own heart the tenets of your own belief; be bold enough to adopt, fearlessly and completely, the attitude of your Creator.

SIXTEEN

Opinions Worthy of a Christian

LET THESE PROPOSITIONS of true Christianity abide with you steadily and permanently: that no Christian should suppose that he was born for himself or should want to live for him-

self, but that whatever he has or is, all this he should attribute
not to himself but to God, the Creator, from whom it came;
and that he should consider all his goods the common
property of all men. Christian love makes no fine distinctions.
Let him love good men in Christ and bad men on account of
Christ, who thus first loved us even while we were His
enemies so that He gave Himself to us wholly for our redemption.[1] Let him value the one kind because they are good, but
cherish these others no less because he may make them good.
Let him, in short, despise no man any more than a reliable
physician would despise the sick. Let him be an enemy only
to wickedness.

The graver the illness, the greater the devotion pure love
will expend upon it. Suppose a man is an adulterer, or a
blasphemer, or a Turk; let the Christian abhor the adultery,
not the man. Let him spurn the blasphemy, not the man. Let
him destroy Turkishness, not the man. Let him take pains that
the evil that person has himself created may perish, but that
the man God has made may be saved. Let him sincerely wish
good, pray for good, act for good to all men.

Let him not injure the deserving and aid the undeserving;
by the same token, let him rejoice in other people's good as
in his own. Let him be as sorry for the misfortunes of other
people as for his own. Surely this is what the Apostle commanded: "To weep with those who weep, and rejoice with
those who rejoice."[2] Indeed, he should suffer more for another's pain than for his own and be happier for a brother's
good than for his own.

This is not the way a Christian should think: "What is he
to me? I do not know whether he's white or black. I do not
know him. He is a stranger. He never did anything for me.
At times he has done me harm, and he has never done me a
favor."

None of this. Remember only how little you deserved the
things Christ did for you, and that He wants you to repay
His goodness, not to Himself, but to your neighbor. Notice

only what that neighbor needs and what you can do. Think only of this: he is your brother in God. You are one in Christ. He is a member of the same body, redeemed by the same blood, comrade in the same faith, called to the same grace and felicity of a life to come.[3]

As the Apostle has put it, "One body and one spirit, just as you have been called in one hope of your calling; one Lord and one faith, one baptism, one God, and Father of all who is above all, in all things, and in all of us."[4] Who can be a stranger when he is linked to you by such a manifest body of unity? Among pagans let those considerations of the rhetoricians carry some weight, if you will, in determining either benevolence or enmity. "He is a fellow citizen, a relative by marriage, a blood relation; or, on the other hand, an acquaintance, my father's friend, a deserving fellow, agreeable, of honorable birth, wealthy," and so on. In Christ either these things are nothing or, as Paul puts it, they are all one and the same.[5]

Let this one point be constantly kept in sight, and let it be enough for you: "He is my flesh, he is my brother in Christ. Does anything granted to the individual member not contribute to the whole body and from thence to the head? We are all mutual members of one another.[6] The united parts make up the body; of that body Jesus Christ is the head, and of Christ God is the head.[7] Whatever is done to you, whatever is done to any member—for good or ill— is done to every one, is done to Christ, is done to God.[8] All these are one: God, Christ, the body, and its members.

Among Christians the old saying "Like with like"[9] does not properly apply, or that other one, "Difference is the mother of hatred." Of what use are the terms of discord where unity is everything? There is no flavor of Christliness in the fact that everywhere courtier is at odds with townsman, rustic with city dweller, patrician with commons, official with private citizen, rich man with poor man, famous with obscure, powerful with weak, Italian with German, Frenchman with Briton, Briton with Scot, grammarian wtih theologian, lawyer with physician, learned with unlearned, eloquent with inarticulate, bachelor with married man, young man with elderly, cleric with layman, priest with monk, Minorite with Colete, Carmelite with Jacobite—not to run through the whole inventory of antagonisms between those who are unlike in quite trifling ways.

Where is that charity which loves even an enemy, when a different surname, a different color of dress, a different belt or shoe or like nonsense of men makes me hateful to you? Why do we not rather give up these childish toys and get in the habit of keeping our eyes on what is pertinent? What this is, Paul teaches us in many passages: that we are all members of one body in Christ our Head,[10] and that inspired by the same spirit we should not envy members more fortunate but should gladly assist those weaker than we; that we can be sure we ourselves have received His blessing when we show kindness to our neighbor; that we have received a hurt when our brother has; that no one should covet anything for himself personally, but that in proportion to his means every man should share in common whatever he has received from God; that all things must return to the source from which they came—namely, God.

This, clearly, is what Paul is writing to the Corinthians. "For just as the body is one though it has many members," he says, "and all the members of the body, even though they are many, nevertheless are of one body, so it is with Christ. For truly we have all been baptized in one Spirit and into one body, whether we are Jews or Gentiles, slaves or freemen, and we have all drunk of one Spirit. For the Body is not one member, but many. If the foot were to say, 'Since I am not a hand, I am not a part of the body,' is it for that reason not a part? If the ear should say, 'I am not an eye; I am not part of the body,' is it for that reason not a part? If the whole body were an eye, where then would be the hearing? If hearing were the whole, where would smelling be? But God has placed the members, every single one of them, in the body just as He wanted them. If they were all the same member, where would be the body? Now, however, we have many members, but only one body. The eye cannot say to the hand, 'I do not need your help,' nor the head to the feet, 'You are not necessary to me.'

"Quite the contrary, those members of the body which seem comparatively feeble are all the more necessary, and what we consider the baser parts of the body, upon them we confer the fuller honor. Our more unseemly parts receive the more abundant attention, whereas our more comely parts have no need. God, however, has suitably arranged the body by assigning the greater distinction to that part where it was lacking, so that there may be no schism in the body, but that individual parts may be mutually solicitous of one another. But it is you who are the body of Christ, members dependent on one another."[11]

In a similar vein he writes to the Romans. "For," he says, "just as we have many members of one body, but not all the members have the same function, so the many of us are one body in Christ, each one a part of every other part and having different gifts according to the grace given us."[12] And also to the Ephesians: "Declaring the truth in love," he says, "let us in all things grow in Him who is Christ, our Head, from whom the whole body, knit and united by every joint's dutiful functioning according to the capacity of each member, produces growth of the body for its glorification in love."[13] And elsewhere he orders us reciprocally to bear one another's burdens, since we are members of one another.[14]

Decide for yourself, then, whether the people you hear everywhere talking in this fashion really belong to this body: "I inherited my property. I possess it by right, not by fraud. Why should I not use it or misuse it as I see fit? Why give anything to those people to whom I owe nothing? If I squander it or waste it, what I lose is mine. It is nobody else's business."

A fellow member starves while you are belching the flesh of partridge. A naked brother shivers while your superfluous clothing goes to waste by moth and dry rot. In one night's dice game you throw away a thousand gold pieces while in the meantime some wretched girl is driven by poverty to prostitute herself; and her soul, for which Christ gave His life, perishes.

"What's that to me?" you say. "I do as I please with what is mine."

And after this, with that kind of attitude, do you still think of yourself as a Christian when you are not even a man?

You listen to this or that person's reputation being sullied in a large company and you keep still, or perhaps you are even amused by the slanderer. "I would have confuted what was said," you claim, "if it had been any business of mine. But he was nothing to me, the fellow being slandered."

Then the body is nothing to you if the member is nothing. Even the Head is nothing to you if the body is nothing.

"It is only just," people say, "to answer force with force."

But I do not care what the law of the authorities permits; I am only astounded that such ideas should have permeated the moral texture of Christian men. "I gave an injury, but only when I was provoked." "I would rather hurt than be hurt." Granted that the laws of man do not punish what they have allowed, but what is Christ, your Chieftain, going to do if you have made a joke of His law found in Matthew? "I say to you, moreover, not to resist an injury, but if anyone should strike you on the right cheek offer him the other; and to him who wishes to take you to law to get your shirt, give your coat also. And if anyone demands a mile of you, go with him two more. Love your enemies and bless those who hate you. Pray for those who persecute you and accuse you falsely, that you may be sons of your Father who is in heaven and who makes His sun rise upon the good and the bad alike and His rain fall upon both the just and the unjust."[15]

"He did not say these things to me," you answer. "He was speaking to the Apostles, to perfect men."

But have you not heard that you are sons of your Father? If you do not want to be a child of God, the law has no application to you; but someone who has no desire to be perfect is not even good. Understand this: if you do not want the reward you are enjoined to nothing, for this point follows: "If you love those who love you, what reward will you have?"[16] That is to say, none at all, since to do that is no virtue: not to do it is a crime. Where like is returned for like, neither owes anything to the other.

Listen to Paul, the great expounder and interpreter of Christian law: "Bless those who persecute you; bless them and do not curse them, returning no one evil for evil. If it can be done, as much as is in your power, dear friends, yield the point to anger and live peaceably with all men, without defending yourselves. For it is written, 'Vengeance is mine, says the Lord.' Therefore, if your enemy is hungry, feed him; if he is thirsty, give him a drink. In doing this you will heap coals of fire upon his head. Do not be overcome by evil, but overcome evil with good."[17]

"Then what is going to happen," you say, "if by my softness I encourage someone else's impudence, and by enduring an old injury invite a new one?"

If you can avoid or ward off an evil without committing one of your own, no one forbids you to do so. But if you cannot, be sure you do not say it is better to do a wrong than to suffer one. If you can, correct your enemy either by overwhelming him with kindness or conquering him with mildness. If this is not possible, better that one should perish than that both should; better that you grow rich in the resources of patience than that both become evil by retaliating in kind.

A Christian, therefore, is commanded to compete with all men only in love, gentleness, and good deeds, and willingly to give over contention, hatred, slander, insults, and injury, even to men of low station.

"But," you say, "the person one may submit to or treat kindly is undeserving."

Even so, it is fitting that you should do it; and Christ, for whose sake you do it, is also worthy.

"I do not want to harm anyone," men say; "neither will I let myself be harmed."

Nevertheless, if you have received an injury, free your mind of it, and take care to avoid doing anything that someone can pay you back for. Be as vigilant in shunning your own faults as in paying off someone else's. The better man you are, the more you will submit to in order to serve everyone in brotherly love.[18] If you are of a distinguished family, the moral values worthy of Christ will not dull but enhance the luster of your race. If you are learned, the more tolerantly you should bear and amend the ignorance of the unlettered. The more debts you acquire, the more obligation you have toward your brother. If you are rich, remember that you are the manager, not the owner, and scrupulously observe how you handle these common goods.[19]

Did you suppose that wealth was forbidden only to monks? Or poverty enjoined only of them? You are wrong: both rules apply to all Christians.[20] The law punishes you if you steal someone else's belongings, but it does not punish you for keeping your own property from a needy brother. Christ, however, will punish both actions.

If you are a magistrate, let your position not make you the more harsh, but your responsibility make you so much the more concerned. "I do not hold a Church office," you say. "I am not a pastor or a bishop."

Granted, but are not you even a Christian? If you are not an ecclesiastic, have a care what camp you are in. To such an extent has Christ won the contempt of the world that they consider no fellowship with Him attractive or pleasing, and the closer the relationship any person has with Him, the more despicable that person is. Every day do not you hear angry non-churchmen hurl the words "clergyman," "priest," and "friar" in our faces as a form of derisive abuse? And this, indeed, with the same spirit and purpose they might accuse one of blasphemy or incest!

As a matter of fact, I cannot imagine why they do not go as far as to object even to baptism, why they do not follow the Saracens in making Christ a synonym for evil. If they were speaking of a bad cleric or an unworthy priest or a disreputable monk, then they might be excused on the grounds that they were criticizing the characters of men, not despising the profession of virtue; but those who pride themselves on defiling virgins, on looting in war, on winning or losing money at dice, find in someone else nothing more abominable or shameful or vile to reproach him with than the names "monk" or "priest." It is not hard, certainly, to see what these men—nominal Christians only—think of Christ.

There is not one Lord for bishops and another for civil officials. Both administer their charges under the same, and to the same both must give an accounting. If you look to any other quarter than Him either in taking up public office or in conducting it, it is not important that the world does not call you a simoniac: be sure that He will punish you as one. If you court public rewards, not for the common good but with an eye to your private gain or to get even with people you have a grudge against, in the eyes of God your magistracy is nothing but freebooting. Let us say that you prosecute thieves, not in order that the man robbed may get back his property but that what the thieves have may not get away from you: how much difference is there between you and them, I ask you, except that they rob the merchants and you rob the robbers?

In short, unless you conduct your office in such a spirit that you are prepared to defend justice at the cost, I shall not say merely of your wealth but even of your life, Christ will not approve your conduct. Let me add Plato's remark that no one who wants office deserves to have it.[21] If you are a prince, take care that the noxious words of flatterers do not bewitch you: "You are a lord and above the law. For you everything goes, everything is honest. You can do whatever you please. What the priests are always harping on to the common people is nothing to you." On the contrary, consider that this is the right of it: Christ Jesus is the one Lord of all. You should emulate as best you can Him whom you actually serve as a deputy. No one should observe His teachings more scrupulously than you, from whom He will exact a more stringent accounting than from others. Do not convince yourself that what you want is bound to be right, but only that you should want the right things. Whatever is wrong for any other mortal man you should consider unfitting for yourself.

Indeed, you should allow less leeway to yourself than is ordinarily condoned by most people. Regard a light misdemeanor in others as a disgrace in yourself. Do not let honor, admiration, reputation, favor, and authority come because you have more money than the common run of people; instead, let your superior moral strength deserve them. Do not let the masses learn to marvel at those things in you which lure them into the mischief you punish every day. Remove this respect for money, and where are the thieves, the embezzlers, the brigands, the plunderers of churches? Take away these plaudits for sensual pleasures, and where are the philanderers and adulterers? Do not make a show of your riches before the eyes of fools every time you want to look somewhat resplendent to your subjects; do not exhibit voluptuousness and self-indulgence every time you want to seem fairly well off.

In yourself first of all let them learn to despise such things and to cherish virtue, to value frugality, to applaud temperance, to honor sobriety. See to it that nothing appears in your behavior which your authority punishes in the behavior of the populace. You will have most effectively reduced evildoing when the provocation of evil-doing, riches and debauchery, are not apparent in you.

You will not scorn any mere plebeian before you; both of you were redeemed at one and the same price. Do not let yourself be guarded from contempt by the clamor of ambition or your severity or your armed attendants, but by your integrity and uprightness of life, and a character untainted by any of the popular vices. Nothing prevents a man assuming leadership from holding the top position, but at the same time, in charity, attaching no importance to being at the top. Think of this as princeliness: to surpass, not in opulence but in the possibilities of service to all men.

Do not turn that which is public property to your own advantage, but lavish your own goods, as well as your whole self, upon the public welfare. If the people owe a great deal to you, you owe everything to Him. If your ear has to listen to ostentatious titles like "Mighty," Most Holy," "Majesty," let your heart not believe in them but attribute all these things to Christ, to whom alone they are appropriate. Let the "crime" of affronted dignity, which others speak of in the voice of Tragedy, be inconsequential as far as you are concerned. The person who truly belittles the majesty of a prince is the one who, in the name of the prince, acts cruelly, iniquitously, harshly, unjustly.

Let no injury affect you less than one which affects you personally. Remember that you are a public figure and that you should not heed anything less than the public good. If you are wise you will keep in mind, not how great you are, but how great a responsibility you carry on your shoulders; and the greater the risk you run, the fewer the concessions you should make to yourself, seeking the pattern for your rule, not from your ancestors or from flatterers, but from Christ. For what is more incongruous than for a Christian prince to set up as a model for himself a Hannibal or an Alexander the Great, a Caesar or a Pompey? When he cannot attain to certain virtues in these men, he will emulate most assiduously the very qualities he ought to have shunned. If Caesar did something praised by the historians, a prince should not forthwith take him as an example, but only if he did something not incompatible with the teachings of our Lord, or of such a nature that, even though it should not be imitated, it may nevertheless stimulate the cultivation of virtue.

Not even a whole empire is great enough that you should be willing to swerve from the right; better to get rid of that than to lose Christ. Make no doubt about it: He has something far better to offer for the empire you have refused. Nothing is so becoming, so splendid, so glorious in kings as to resemble as closely as possible Jesus, the King of all, who just as He was greatest, was also best. But He concealed here on earth the fact that He was greatest, preferring that we understand instead the fact that He was best, since his quality was what He wishes us to emulate. He denied that His kingdom was of this world, although He was Master of heaven and earth.[22]

The rulers of this world exercise power over those they rule, but a Christian does not apply power to his people, but love. He who is greatest of all considers himself servant of all, not master.[23] For this reason I am all the more astonished at the arrogant terms of authority and dominion being applied even to our chief priests and bishops, at our divines' —no less foolishly than pretentiously—not being ashamed to be called "masters" by the common people, even though Christ forbade his followers to permit themselves to be called either "masters" or "lords"; for Christ Jesus, the Head of us all, is both the sole Master and the sole Lord.[24] "Apostle," "pastor," "bishop" are terms of service, not rule; "pope," and "abbott" are words of love, not dominion.

But why launch out into that sea of vulgarian error? According to whatever type of men he examines, a truly spiritual man will see many things everywhere he can laugh at, more that he can weep for; he will see a great many opinions so radically corrupted as to have no resemblance to the teaching of Christ, from which a good part of them were derived, for even into Christianity we have introduced a certain worldliness. That which is read about the "world" in the very early theologians, badly educated people today apply only to those who are not monks. In the Gospel, however, and in the Apostles, in Augustine, Ambrose, and Jerome, the "world" refers to unbelievers, blasphemers against God, the enemies of the cross of Christ. People of this sort are anxious about tomorrow; obviously they have no faith in Christ if they contend fiercely for money, for power, for pleasure, as is natural in those who have been blinded by the illusion of sense experience and who value seeming goods in place of real ones.

For this world has not known Christ, the true Light. Wholly set on evil, it loves self, lives for self, works for self because it has not taken up the true love of Christ.[25] From this world Christ separated not only the Apostles but all those whom He judged worthy. How then can we blend this world, everywhere damned in Holy Scripture, with Christianity? How can we prettify our vices with the terminology of an empty worldliness? A great many learned men spread this sickness, adulterating the Word of God and, as Paul says, corrupting Holy Scripture in accordance with the moral temper of the times when it would be more appropriate to amend morality by the principles of Scripture.[26]

No sort of flattery is more deadly, really, than to rationalize a spiritual malady, not heal it, with passages from the Gospel or the prophets. A prince hears it said that "all power is from God,"[27] and immediately he begins to preen himself.[28] Now why has the Scripture made you more arrogant than uneasy? Do you think God has given you power to administer and that He does not also demand an accounting of the way you administer that power?[29] A miser hears that Christians are forbidden to have two coats,[30] and a clergyman offers the interpretation that a second coat exceeds the requirement of nature and contributes to the sin of covetousness.

"Fine!" says this stupid fellow. "There are many things I do not own!"

A man naturally brutish and lacking in charity hears that the proper sequence of charity is to value your own life before another's, your own money, your own reputation.

"Well, then," he says, "I will give nothing, lest I myself should be without. I will not defend *his* good name, lest some spot should fall on my own. I will abandon a brother in danger to avoid running any risk myself. In short, I will live completely for myself so that I will not get into trouble over someone else."

We have also learned from saintly men that if they have done anything unfit to be imitated, we set up that thing alone as a model for our behavior. Adulterers and murderers justify themselves by the example of David.[31] Those who pant for a fat purse offer the wealth of Abraham[32] as their excuse. Princes whose general sport is the defloration of virgins enumerate for us the queens and concubines of Solomon.[33] Those whose god is the belly bring up in extenuation the drunkenness of Noah.[34] The incestuous defend their vileness with the coupling of Lot and his daughters.[35]

Why do we look to these examples and away from Christ? I say unequivocally that not even the prophets or the Apostles should be made our models if they deviate in any way from the instruction of Christ, but if we are to follow these saintly sinners I do not protest, except to object to their not being followed in every way. If you have made David your pattern in adultery, make David more especially your pattern in penitence. If you have copied Magdalene the sinner, copy also her great love, her tears, her humbling herself at the feet of Jesus.[36] If you have persecuted the Church of God, as Paul did,[37] and perjured yourself, as Peter did,[38] see to it that like Paul you offer your life for the sake of your faith and that like Peter you do not cringe away from the cross.

Thus God allows great men to slip into certain errors so that when we err we may not despair but, just as we have been their companions in sinning, so we may be the same in correcting our sins. Now we magnify the very thing we should not follow and distort certain things they did virtuously, like spiders extracting whatever poison is present or even turning wholesome medicine into mischief. What do the riches of Abraham have to do with you, whose Deity is dividends? Because, with God favoring his affairs, he was enriched by the increase of his flocks—and this only in terms of carnal law—is it for that reason permissible for you, a Christian, to heap up by hook or crook the wealth of a Croesus which you will either squander wickedly or hide more wickedly at home? Even when riches were pouring in of their own accord, he did not fix his mind on them, as is shown by the fact that when the voice of God ordered him he at once produced his only son to be sacrificed.[39] How much do you think he prized a herd of cattle when he disregarded even his own son? And you, then, who dream of nothing but profit, who care for nothing but money, who are ready to cheat your own brother or forsake Christ the moment the prospect of a little cash presents itself—do you think you are anything like Abraham?

The ingenuous daughters of Lot, seeing the whole area aflame in every direction, thinking this was the whole world which they were looking at and that from such a vast conflagration no mortal creature had survived except themselves, secretly managed sexual relations with their father. This they did, however, not lustfully but with commendable intentions: that every trace of humankind might not vanish, especially when the divine injunction to increase and multiply was still very cogent. And do you have the effrontery to compare your ravenous sensuality with the action of these girls?

As a matter of fact, I would unhesitatingly excuse your wedlock less than their incest if, in marriage, you aim not at having children but at gratifying your lusts.

After offering so many examples of virtue, David succumbed to adultery one time when the occasion presented itself without his seeking it. Does it follow that you will be permitted to tumble about as you please in other men's beds all your life?

In mortal fear Peter once denied Christ, for whom he was later going to die; is it right, then, for you to perjure yourself for whatever reason you think convenient? Paul sinned, not through passion, but mistaken conviction; once warned, he came to his senses. Are you growing old in wickedness knowingly, deliberately, with your eyes wide open and, using Paul as an excuse, patting yourself on the head? Matthew, at one word of command, unhesitatingly gave up all his tax collection.[40] Are you so addicted to money that all these examples of saintly men, all the sermons and gospels you have heard cannot woo you away from it?

Bishops tell me that Saint Augustine had two mistresses. He, however, was educated as a pagan, we as Christians. And he did this in his youth, whereas we do it as graybeards. An extraordinary comparison, seeing that as a young man and a pagan, in order to avoid the snares of marriage, he kept one little wench instead of a wife and gave her the loyalty of a husband even though she was not his wife![41] Will it be less reprehensible, then, for us—Christian men, old men, priests, bishops!—to befoul ourselves in every hog wallow of lust?

Morality is in a bad way when we have given vices the names of virtues and become more clever at excusing our sins than diligent in amending them, especially if we have learned how to feed and nourish our depraved notions with specious apologetics drawn from holy Scripture. Therefore, my dearest brother, rejecting the world totally and sincerely in all its opinions and deeds, seize unequivocally upon the Christian way. Disregard whatever is accessible to the senses in this life, whether repugnant or appealing, in favor of an imperturbable love of goodness. Let Christ, the only source both of true understanding and a happy life, be enough for you. This, of course, the world considers pure madness and folly; but through it God is pleased to save those who believe.[42] He is happily a fool who is wise in Christ, miserably a fool who does not know Him.

But take note of this. Though I want you to differ stoutly from the world, I do not want you to take up a kind of churlish cynicism, attacking the opinions of everyone else, superciliously damning everything, hatefully railing at everyone else, viciously slurring every kind of life. This would be to acquire two evils for yourself at the same time; first, you would end up being hated by everyone; and, second, being hated you would be of no good to anyone. When it is not at odds with virtue to do so, be all things to all men so that you may gain men for Christ.[43] Adapt yourself to all men outwardly, as long as your resolution remains firm inwardly. Externally, let gentleness, affability, friendliness, agreeableness influence your brother; better pleasantly to draw him to Christ than to repel him with your asperity. In sum, you ought to express what you believe in by your moral habits rather than by issuing proclamations in abusive language. But, again, do not cater to popular frailties in such a way that you do not dare to stand up doughtily for truth when the occasion demands. Men should be improved by your humanity, not misled by it.

SEVENTEEN

The Seventh Rule

(Training in the Practice of Virtue)

FURTHERMORE, IF THE weakness and frailty of our nature make it impossible for us to attain that spiritual state, nevertheless we must not slack off one bit in our effort to come as near to it as possible. For that matter, the true and easy way to felicity is this: once we have thus turned our whole mind to the contemplation of things divine, just as the body is attended by its shadow, so the love of Christ and the love of things eternal and good is naturally attended by an aversion for things transitory, a hatred for things vile. The one necessarily accompanies the other, and each flourishes or dwindles with the other. To the extent that you increase in the love of Christ, to that extent you will hate the world. The more you marvel at things unseen, the less value you will set upon things fleeting and nugatory. We should therefore, as Fabius counsels, train ourselves in the practice of virtue as we do in literary studies, by steadily straining toward the highest excellence.[1]

If this is incompatible with our deficiencies, the next best thing is to abstain, with a certain natural caution, from the major vices so that we may, as far as we can, keep ourselves whole for God's good services. Just as the body is nearer health when, even though exhausted and wasted, it is yet free of noxious humors, so the mind is more receptive to God's munificence when it is not yet polluted by heinous offenses, even if it as yet lacks true virtue. If we are too weak to emulate the Apostles or the martyrs or virgins, at least let us not be guilty of seeming to be outstripped by pagans in this contest. For many of them, even though they knew no God they should revere, or believed in no hell they should fear, nevertheless thought everyone should avoid baseness for its own sake, so much so that some of them preferred to give up fame, wealth, and life itself rather than part with honor.

If sin in itself is such that it should not be countenanced for any conceivable advantage or because of any conceivable disadvantage, surely even if God's justice does not terrify or His mercy dissuade him, if neither hope of eternal life nor fear of eternal punishment puts him off, if not even the inherent nastiness repellent to pagans is repellent to him, at least the thousand ills which attend the sinner even in this life ought to deter him—infamy, waste of property, penury, contempt and scorn on the part of good men, uneasiness of mind, perturbation, and that most painful torture of a guilty conscience which, even if many people do not experience it now in the dull insensitivity of youth or the intoxication of pleasurable sin, they will nevertheless experience later on. And the later they do it, the more keenly by far.

So young men should be very powerfully admonished, so that they will prefer to take the word of the very many commentators that such is the nature of sin rather than learn for themselves by costly experience and spoil their lives with vice before they have clearly understood what life really is. If you put little value in Christ, upon whom you are dependent for so much, at least you should abstain from depravity for your own sake. And though it is very dangerous to loiter too long in this situation—at the crossroads, so to speak— nevertheless, for those who cannot yet attain to virtue of heroic proportions it is not a little preferable to take a stand in politic morality rather than plunge headlong into all sorts of baseness. This is not the ultimate in felicity, but it is a step nearer to it. In the meantime, however, we must always pray to God that He will deign to raise us up to nobler things.

EIGHTEEN

The Eighth Rule

(The Value of Temptation)

IF THE WINDS of temptation buffet you rather frequently and heavily, do not immediately begin to fret, as if for this reason God did not care for you, or you were out of favor with Him, or not good enough or the less devout. On the contrary, be grateful that He is instructing His future heir just as He chastises a very dear son or tests a friend.[1] The best evidence that a person has been rejected by divine mercy is that he is assailed by no temptation. Remember the Apostle Paul, who was worthy of admission to the mysteries of the third circle of heaven but who nevertheless was buffeted by the messenger of Satan.[2] Think of Job, the friend of God; think of Jerome, of Benedict, of Francis, and along with these a countless number of the other holy fathers plagued by the gravest sins. If what you endure is common to so many men, and such great ones, what reason for you to be downhearted? Exert yourself all the more, so that you may triumph as they did. God will not fail you; along with temptation He will also provide the way for you to resist it.[3]

NINETEEN

The Ninth Rule

(Vigilance against Sin)

JUST AS EXPERIENCED generals are in the habit of keeping alert even in quiet periods, so you too should always be vigilant, watchful for any future assault of the adversary (for he never ceases to travel about, looking for someone to devour[1]), that you may be better prepared to repel him stoutly at the very moment he attacks you, and grind under your heel the head of that poisonous serpent.[2] For on no occasion is he more easily, or more completely, conquered. It is a very good idea, therefore, to dash these young progeny of Babylon upon the rock which is Christ just as soon as they are born, and before they have a chance to grow up.[3]

TWENTY

The Tenth Rule

(The Weapons of Prayer, Holy Scripture, and Maxims)

THE TEMPTER IS best repulsed, however, by these methods:[1] by completely shunning him in spirit and immediately spitting out his promptings; by ardent prayer; by applying yourself wholeheartedly to some wholesome activity; or by trying to answer the tempter with the words of Holy Scripture, as we have already suggested so many times. In this respect, indeed, having ready certain maxims against every type of temptation will be of no little help, especially those which have at some time or other deeply stirred your heart.

TWENTY-ONE

The Eleventh Rule

(Trust Not Yourself but Christ)

VIRTUOUS MEN ARE chiefly beset by two dangers: one, that they may succumb to temptation; two, that in overcoming temptation they may grow smug in spiritual complacency and self-righteousness. That you may escape not only the terror by night, therefore, but also the demon that works at high noon,[1] see to it that when the enemy solicits you to evil you have no concern for your own frailty but remember only this: you are equal to anything through Christ,[2] who said, not only to the Apostles but to you as well and to all His members, however weak, "Have faith, for I have overcome the world."[3]

Again, when you have overcome the tempter, or when in some pious occupation you perceive your mind to be privately reveling in a kind of self-congratulation, then be constantly on guard; do not attribute anything of this sort to your own merits but consider that you have received it all through the gratuitous beneficence of God. And restrain yourself always with the words of Paul: "What do you have that has not been given to you? And if you have been given it, why should you be puffed up, as if you had not been given it?"[4]

So, against this double evil a double remedy: first, distrustful of your own moral strength, take refuge in Christ, your Head, and place all hope of victory in His benevolence alone; and, second, give thanks steadily for spiritual comfort, humbly acknowledging to Him your own unworthiness of His goodness.

TWENTY-TWO

The Twelfth Rule

(Be Not Content Merely to Resist Sin;
Strive for Perfect Virtue)

WHEN YOU FIGHT with the enemy, do not be satisfied with
evading his strokes or even with thrusting him back, but
manfully turning against the foe himself the weapon you
have seized, cut him down with his own blade. You will do
this when you not only do not yield to temptation but make
it an occasion for developing virtue. And just as the poets
sensibly represent Hercules as toughening in courage
through the perils a wrathful Juno imposed upon him, so you
too should try not only to avoid becoming worse as a result
of the adversary's devices, but even to come out a better
man than before.

If you are inflamed by lust, acknowledge your weakness
and deny yourself somewhat more, even of lawful pleasures;
assign yourself an additional number of chaste and moral
duties. If you are enticed by greed or avarice, increase your
charitable donations. If you are attracted by empty fame,
humble yourself that much more in every respect. Thus it
will happen that along with every temptation you will have
a certain revitalization of holy purpose and a renewal of devotion. No other method is so continually effective in subduing and overthrowing the foe, for he will be afraid to provoke you again lest he who rejoices in being the author of
badness should instead provide the occasion for goodness.

TWENTY-THREE

The Thirteenth Rule

(Have Hope in Final Victory but Be Ever on Guard)

MOREOVER, YOU SHOULD always fight with this attitude and hope, that if you come off the winner, this battle will be your last. For it can happen that divine mercy will grant such a prize to your virtue that once the enemy has been ignominiously routed he will never again hunt you out, something we read of in connection with certain holy men. Nor is it foolish of Origen to think that when Christians are victorious the power of their foes is lessened and that once Satan has been stoutly repulsed he is never permitted to return to the assault.[1]

In strife, then, dare to hope for lasting peace. But, again, after you have won, conduct yourself as if you would soon renew the fight. You should always expect one trial after another and never lay down your arms, never leave your post, never relax your guard as long as you serve in this garrison of the body. In his heart everyone should always carry that declaration of the prophet: "I will stand my guard."[2]

TWENTY-FOUR

The Fourteenth Rule

(Take No Vice Lightly)

BE ESPECIALLY CAREFUL not to take any vice lightly, as if it were of no consequence, for no enemy has won more often than one who has been disregarded. In this respect I have found not a few men pitiably deceived: they deceive themselves as long as they wink at one fault or another of their own, each man gently excusing his own habits while at the same time he vehemently deplores all the rest. A large part of those whom the common run of men call upright and uncorrupted roundly detest theft, pillage, murder, adultery, and incest; but simple fornication and a modest excursion into sensuality they by no means shun, thinking all this inconsequential. One man, moral enough in other respects, is too fond of the bottle and given to excess. Another is too bawdy a talker. Still another is rather vain and boastful.

In the long run, what sin will we do without if everyone indulges his own in this fashion? This situation argues that such people do not actually possess the other virtues if any vice at all pleases them, but instead certain semblances of virtue which either nature, or training, or custom (save the mark!) gave even to the characters of the pagans.

A man who hates any vice with Christian hatred must hate them all; as soon as real charity takes over his heart, he attacks the whole cohort of evils with impartial dislike and does not even coddle himself with the trivial ones for fear that he may slide imperceptibly from these little ones into the bigger ones and while being lax about trifles miss the most essential. And though you may not be able as yet to pull up all your sins by the roots, you ought at least to pluck away one or another of your bad qualities and add something, always, to your moral resources. In this manner that great heap of Hesiod will either grow or dwindle.[1]

TWENTY-FIVE

The Fifteenth Rule

(Keep in Mind the Future—the Bitterness of Sin;
the Sweetness of Victory)

IF THE STRUGGLE one has to undergo in the conflict with
temptation alarms you, this will be a help: do not contrast
the grimness of the fight with the pleasantness of the sin, but,
instead, the present bitterness of struggle with the future
bitterness of sin which awaits him who is defeated. Then
compare the present sweetness of sin, which attracts you,
with the future sweetness of victory and the peace of mind
awaiting him who has fought vigorously, and you will soon
see what an unequal comparison it is.

People who are not careful enough in this respect are deceived, because they compare the disagreeableness of the
contest with the agreeableness of the sin, nor do they consider the consequences of the one or the other. For a distress
comes to the vanquished which is both deeper and longer
lasting than he would have had if he had won his fight; likewise a greater and more lasting pleasure comes to the victor
than that which drew the loser into sin, a fact which one who
has put both courses to the proof will easily ascertain. Certainly no Christian should be so consistently craven that even
though he daily succumbs to temptation he does not care to
find out what it would be like to overcome it. The oftener he
will do this, the sweeter will become his victory.

TWENTY-SIX

The Sixteenth Rule

(Meet Defeat with Renewed Effort)

BUT IF AT some time you should suffer a critical wound, be sure you do not drop your shield and weapons and straightway capitulate to the foe, something I have seen happen to many people whose spirit was naturally somewhat flabby and soft, so that when they had once been bowled over they stopped fighting and gave themselves over completely to sensual passions without thought of recovering their freedom. Very dangerous is such pusillanimity, which is sometimes typical of characters not really very bad but prone to succumb to that worst of all mental states—despair. Against this weakness, therefore, we must fortify our minds with this rule: that if we stumble into error we not only should not give up hope but should emulate tough soldiers, whom not infrequently the fear of dishonor and the pain of a wound not only does not put to flight but even spurs and stimulates to fight more fiercely than ever.

As soon as we have fallen into mortal danger, then, we too should hasten to screw up our courage, and when we have ignominiously failed, make amends with a new impetuosity of virtue. You will heal one wound more easily than many, a fresh one more easily than one old and already festering. Encourage yourself with that well-known line Demosthenes is said to have used: "The man in flight will fight again."[1] Think of the prophet David, of King Solomon, of Peter, prince of the Church, of the Apostle Paul: think into what baseness such luminaries of holiness fell and that God perhaps allowed them to fall for this reason—that if you fell you would not despair.

Get on your feet, then, and return to the fight at once with a stout heart, not only the more eagerly but the more warily. Sometimes it happens that the grievous sins committed by good men are converted into a mountain of goodness when they who erred the most shamefully love the more fervently.

TWENTY-SEVEN

The Seventeenth Rule

(The Mystery of the Cross)

AGAINST VARIOUS AND sundry onslaughts of the tempter, however, various and sundry remedies are useful. Nevertheless, against every kind of adversity or temptation the cross of Christ is by far the one most potent. It is at once an example to the erring, a comfort to the hard-pressed, and armor for those who fight. It is the only defense to be used against the whole assortment of weapons of our most wicked enemy.

Accordingly, it is safest to exercise yourself diligently in its use, though not, of course, after the manner of the vulgar when they repeat daily the story of the Lord's Passion, or pray to a crucifix, or barricade their bodies on all sides with a thousand replicas of it, or preserve some piece of that hallowed wood at home, or at specified hours recollect the suffering of Christ in such a way that they weep and wail with natural human feeling—as they would for some just man who did not deserve his suffering. This is not the real nurture of the Cross, though it may serve for a while as milk for souls still in their spiritual infancy.[1]

You, of course, should climb up into the palm tree to grasp its real harvest.[2] These are the important fruits: that by mor-

tifying the fleshly passions which are our members here on
earth we take pains to fashion these members in conformity
to the Head, a process which not only should not be distasteful to us but even vastly enjoyable and delightful, if only
Christ's spirit lives in us.[3] For who truly loves someone
whom he wants to resemble as little as possible?

Nevertheless, in order that you may with greater profit
meditate upon the mystery of the Cross, it will be necessary
for each one to prepare a certain method for himself, a certain strategy of battle, and to practice it diligently, so that
it may be available whenever the situation demands. The
strategy may be of this sort, that in crucifying each of your
passions you make use of that part of the Cross which works
best, for there is no temptation or adversity whatever that
does not have its own peculiar cure in the Cross.

For instance, when the ambition of this world excites you,
or when you are shamed by derision and mockery, remind
yourself thus: "Oh, vile member! How great is Christ, your
Head, and how he humbled himself for your sake!" When
the evil spirit of envy assails you, remember how gently, how
guilelessly He sacrificed Himself for our sake, how good He
was, even to the worst sinners. When you are drawn by gluttony, remember that He drank gall and vinegar. When you
are moved by filthy voluptuousness, remember how the
whole life of your Lord was free from such pleasures, how it
was full of every hardship and pain and distress. When anger inflames you, let yourself be reminded of Him who was
mute as a lamb in the presence of the shearer and opened
not His mouth.[4] If poverty galls you badly, or the lust of possession agitates you, then put your mind on that Lord of the
universe, who was made so poor for your sake that He had
no place to lay His head.[5]

And if you employ this same method in dealing with your
other temptations, not only will it not be a bitter experience
to have your passions assault you, but even pleasurable; for

you will learn in that way to emulate your Captain and to give thanks, indeed, for those boundless griefs which He suffered for your sake.

TWENTY-EIGHT

The Eighteenth Rule

(The Nobility of Man)

As A MATTER of fact, although this remedy is by far the best of all for those people who go along life's road in the normal fashion, it is nevertheless somewhat useful, too, to the comparatively weak if, when the passions lure them toward wrongdoing they at once call to mind how filthy, how execrable, how deadly a thing sin is, and, on the other hand, how great is the dignity of man.

In trivial matters we deliberate for some time; in this, the most vital of all concerns, before we put ourselves under contract to Satan, so to speak, shall we not recollect what a great Creator made us, for what a lofty state He intended us, at what tremendous cost He redeemed us and to what bliss He has invited us? Shall we not reflect that man is that noblest of creatures for whose sake God framed this marvelous engine of the world, that he is the fellow of angels, the son of God, heir of eternal life, member of Christ and of the Church; that our bodies are temples of the Holy Spirit, our minds at once the images and secret dwelling places of divinity?[1]

And on the other hand shall we not keep in mind that sin is the most loathsome of diseases, a plague to both mind and body? Innocence restores both to their original splendor, whereas the contagion of sin wastes them away, even in this temporal life. Sin is the deadly venom of that most foul serpent; it is pledge money to the Devil, a guarantee of servitude not only most shameful but most wretched. When you think of the things of this world, constantly ask yourself whether, for the sake of the spurious, transient, and poisonous gratifications of sin, it makes sense to plunge into such degradation, from which you are powerless to rescue yourself.

TWENTY-NINE

The Nineteenth Rule

(Between God and Satan)

THEN COMPARE THOSE two dissimilar Creators, God and Satan, one of whom you make your enemy by sinning and the other your master. Through innocence and grace you join the number of God's friends and are received into the titles and rights of inheritance of His children.[1] Through sin, on the other hand, you are made the slave and son of the Devil.[2] One is that eternal fountain, that Idea of highest beauty, highest pleasure, highest good which is accessible to all. The other is the father of all badness, of utter shame and deepest unhappiness.

Think of the blessing you have received from one, the afflictions from the other. Remember with what goodness God created you, with what mercy He redeemed you, with what freedom He enriched you, with what lenity He daily suffers your lapses, with what rejoicing He welcomes you when come to your senses. As opposed to all this, consider with what malice the Devil long ago plotted against your safety, into what troubles he has got you. And ask yourself, also, what he is working for every day but to drag the whole human race down with him into everlasting perdition.

When you have pondered all of these points pro and con, ask yourself this question. "Shall I, heedless of my origin, heedless of such great blessings, ungratefully cut myself off from so excellent, so loving, so worthy a parent, and for the sake of a bit of trifling and meretricious pleasure voluntarily put myself in the hands of the most cruel and debased master? Shall I not at least do as much for Him as I would do for a mere man, if he was deserving? Shall I not flee the other as I would flee a man if he was intent on doing me harm?"

THIRTY

The Twentieth Rule

(Between Virtue and Sin)

AND INDEED THE prizes are no less unequal than the prize-givers are unlike. For what sharper contrast exists than that between eternal death and immortality, between endless enjoyment of the highest good as a part of the fellowship of heaven and endless suffering of direst torments in the wretched company of the damned? Anyone who is unclear upon this point is not even a man, let alone a Christian. Anyone who does not give it a thought is madder than madness itself.

Besides all this, virtue and sin bear fruits radically dissimilar, for from the one stems serenity and peace of mind and that blissful joy of a clear conscience. Once a man has tasted this, the world has nothing so precious or so gratifying that he would be willing to exchange. On the other hand, the alternative course is attended not only by a thousand other ills but also by that cruelest torture of a guilty conscience. For what Christ has promised in the Gospel is that hundred-fold spiritual joy, a kind of pledge, as it were, of eternal felicity.[1]

These are the marvelous gifts spoken of by the Apostle, which eye has not seen and ear has not heard, and which have not penetrated the heart of man, gifts which God has prepared in this life, surely, for those who love Him,[2] while in the meantime the worm of the wicked does not die[3] and they go through their hell even while they live. Nor is it any other flame in which the rich glutton of the Gospel is tortured,[4] nor any other punishment of the damned about whom the poets have written so much, but the perpetual agony of mind which attends the practice of sin.

Let anyone who wishes, therefore, disregard the various rewards of a life to come: there inheres in virtue itself something abundantly worth seeking, and in vice something he ought to find repellent.

THIRTY-ONE

The Twenty-First Rule

(The Impermanence of Life)

AND CONSIDER THESE things: how troubled, how impermanent is this life, how ever-present is the threat of death, how everywhere he catches us when we least expect him. When no one is safe even for a moment of his life, how great is the danger of protracting that kind of life in which, as often happens, if sudden death surprises you, you have perished everlastingly.

THIRTY-TWO

The Twenty-Second Rule

(Impenitence the Worst of Sins)

IMPENITENCE, THEN, IS always to be dreaded as the worst of all sins, especially if a man considers how few of such a multitude of sinners truly and sincerely come to their senses, particularly those who have dragged along the cords of their vices[1] clear up to the end of their lives. Smooth and easy indeed is the slope down into wickedness,

> But to retrace your steps, climb back to upper air,
> This is a task, this is hard work.[2]

So, take a cue from the mishap of Aesop's goat,[3] and remember before you descend into the pit of sin that the return will not be so easy.

THIRTY-THREE

Remedies for Some Specific Sins and, First of All, for Lust

THUS FAR, OF course, we have been pointing out as well as we could general defenses against any and all types of sins. Now we are going to try to pass on certain tactics of a more specialized nature, showing how you ought to cope with a particular sin. And first of all we shall treat of lust, compared to which no evil attacks us earlier, pricks us more sharply, covers more territory, or drags more people to ruin. Therefore, if filthy sensuality inflames your mind, remember to counter it at once with these weapons.

First of all, think how foul, how base, how unworthy of any man is this pleasure which reduces us from an image of divinity to the level, not merely of animals, but even to that of swine, he goats, dogs, and the most brutish of brutes. Indeed, how far below the status of beast it debases us who were intended to be consorts of angels and have communion with God. Along with these reflections, consider how transient this pleasure is, how spurious, always containing more gall than honey. Conversely, think what a noble thing is the soul, how sacred a thing is the human body, as we have already pointed out in the preceding rules. What stupid folly, then, to pollute simultaneously both soul and body with ignoble habits for the sake of a trifling and filthy titillation of momentary pleasure, to profane the temple Christ has consecrated with His own blood.

Think also of what a vast troop of evils this seductive disease carries with it. First of all it plucks away reputation, that most precious of possessions, for no vice's notoriety stinks worse than that of lechery. It drains away one's patrimony. It destroys at the same time the vigor and attractiveness of the body. It damages health and produces countless ailments, all of them disgusting. It deforms the flowering of youth and hastens a repulsive old age. It does away with the energy of talent, blunts the keenness of the mind, and ingrafts, as it were, a brutish mentality. It repeatedly calls one away from all honorable pursuits and wholly immerses the man, however great, in filth, so that he can think of nothing but the sordid, the base, the vile. The thing that befitted a man, the use of reason, it obliterates. It makes youth crazy, disreputable, besotted and offensive; old age, odious and wretched.

Be sensible, then, and reason it out step by step: "Such and such pleasure turned out so disappointingly, produced so much grief, so much shame, boredom, trouble and disease. Shall I be fool enough knowingly to swallow the hook once more? Shall I do again something that will cause me more grief?"

In the same fashion temper yourself with examples of other men you know who have pursued self-indulgence dishonorably and disastrously. Conversely, stiffen your continence by the numerous examples of young men and tender virgins: reproach your own moral cowardice under comparable circumstances. Why should you be able to do less than such and such persons, of such and such sex and age, of such

and such birth and training have been, and are, able to do?
Have as much love as they, and you will be no less valiant.
Consider how noble, how pleasant, how beautiful is purity
of mind and body. This is what especially makes us the inti-
mates of angels, capable of receiving the Holy Spirit; for certainly that Spirit, as a lover of chastity, recoils from no sin
as it does from lust. It is never so delightedly at home as in
the minds of virgins.

And imagine to yourself just how ridiculous, how completely monstrous it is to be in love: to grow pale and thin,
to shed tears, to fawn upon and play the cringing beggar to
the most stinking tart, to croak and howl at her doors all
night, to hang upon the nod of a mistress, to endure a silly
woman's dominating you, bawling you out, flying at you in
rage, and then to make up with her and voluntarily offer
yourself to a strumpet so she can play upon you, clip you,
pluck you clean! Where, I ask you, in all such behavior is the
name of a man? Where's your beard? Where is that high
mind fashioned for the most beautiful things?

Remind yourself of what a flock of crimes voluptuousness
customarily brings with it, once it takes over. In other vices,
perhaps, there is some resemblance to certain virtues, but
none in lust; it is always coupled with the greatest and most
frequent sins. Supposing it were an inconsequential matter
to go wenching, it is still a grave one not to listen to your parents, to neglect your friends, to squander the family property, to ravish what is another man's, to perjure yourself, to
carouse around, to rob, to become a vicious criminal, to
brawl, commit murder, blaspheme—into all of which and
even worse Madam Lechery will draw you unexpectedly;
and once you have proffered your miserable neck to her
halter, you cease to be your own master.

Besides this, ponder the fact that this life is more evanes-
cent than smoke, emptier than a shadow;[1] think how many
snares death lays for us, lurking in ambush at all times and

in all places. It will be of no little help to recall expressly
those people of your acquaintance whom death seized unexpectedly—members of your family, your peers, or even your
juniors—especially those whom you once had as companions
in sensual pleasure. Thus you may learn to be more wary by
means of another's peril. Think how pleasantly they spent
their lives, but how bitterly they left them, how tardily they
came to their senses and began to hate their own fatal de-
baucheries. Think of the grimness of the Last Judgment and
of the fearful thunderbolt of that irrevocable pronouncement
that sends the wicked into everlasting fire;[2] remember that
these temporal delights, these brief and insubstantial pleasures, must be paid for by eternal torments.

At this point carefully note the balance of the scales: what
an uneven exchange it is, for the sake of the briefest and dirt-
iest kind of wantonness to give up in this life a sweeter and
finer joy of the mind as well as never-ending joys in the life to
come; and to obtain, moreover, everlasting grief in return
for such nugatory little gratifications. Then, if it seems hard
for you to reject so little satisfaction for the sake of Christ,
recollect what tortures He underwent out of love for you.
Besides the miseries common to all human life, what a quan-
tity of His holy blood He shed for your sake, how ignomin-
ious and cruel a death He died for you while you, heedless
of all these things, again crucify the Son of God as you repeat those mad pleasures which brought such sufferings
upon your Master and Lord!

Then, according to the rule set out above, recall how many
blessings He has heaped upon you, none of them yet deserved, in return for all of which, although no part can be
paid for in kind, He nevertheless asks for nothing more than
that you follow His example in fortifying your spirit against
deadly enticements and converting it to the love of the highest good and beauty. Compare those two Venuses and Cu-

THIRTY-THREE: REMEDIES FOR SOME SINS   *181*

pids of Plato: honorable love and sensual, that is, divine pleasure and lustful.[3] Contrast the unlike stuff of each, their dissimilar natures and rewards.

And in every temptation, indeed, but especially when you are lured toward sensuality, visualize your angelic guardian, who is the tireless observer and witness of everything you do or even think about;[4] a god always observant, to whose eyes all things are open, who sits above the heavens and looks into the depths.[5] And surely if you are ashamed to do something nasty in the presence of a mere man, should you not fear to do it in the presence of the angel most like God, and with the whole troop of heaven looking on and execrating the deed? Think, too—as is the case—that if you had eyes sharper than those of a lynx or an eagle, nevertheless, in the brightest light you could not see more clearly what a man is doing right in front of you than God and His angels can see into all the secret nooks and crannies of your mind.

You should also consider the fact that when you yield to lust one of two things will happen: either that, once pleasure has been tasted, it will cloud and beguile your reason in such a way that you will proceed from one nastiness to another until you blindly arrive at a depraved state of consciousness and, hardened in evil, cannot leave off sordid pleasure even when it has already left you in the lurch—something we see happen in many cases, as when with worn out bodies, raddled looks, chilled blood, wasted powers, rheumy eyes, men still itch without ceasing and are more scandalously obscene in their talk than they were once shameless in practice. What can be more monstrous and deplorable than this condition?

Or, the other alternative, that if perchance—through God's special grace—you come to your senses, you must atone for that fleeting and short-lived pleasure with the utmost grief of mind, with profoundest efforts and countless tears. How much more reasonable, therefore, never to admit the virus of carnal indulgence at all than to be seduced into such abominable blindness or to pay for such a paltry and spurious bit of fun with so much distress.

Surely you can apply many things from your own personal circumstances which will be able to deter you from sensuality. If you are a priest, remember that you have dedicated yourself wholly to divine matters. How unworthy and disgraceful it is to touch the disgusting flesh of a whore with that same mouth in which you receive the body of Him so worthy of honor, to handle loathesome filth with the same hands you use—with even the angels participating!—to celebrate that ineffable Mystery. Think how incongruous it is to become one body and one spirit with God—and one body with a tart.[6]

If you are learned, think how much nobler, how much more like God's is your mind, and so much the more incompatible with such contumacy. If you are a noble, a prince, the more conspicuous the disgrace, the more grave the offense. If you are married, think how admirable a thing is an undefiled bed, and try as hard as you can to make your marriage resemble the most holy wedlock of Christ and His Church, whose likeness it bears.[7] That is to say, see to it that it has as little lewdness as possible and as much fruitfulness, for in no status of life is it not most abominable to be a slave to lust.

If you are a young man, guard continually against your recklessly besmutting the flower of youth, which will never come again; against corrupting your best and truly golden years, which flit away appallingly fast and never return; against doing something now, in the ignorance and heedlessness of youth, which will hurt you all the rest of your life with a nagging consciousness of misdeeds and with those painful stings that fleeting pleasure leaves in our minds. If you are a woman, remember that nothing more becomes your sex than modesty; if you are a man, that you are that

much better fitted for excellence and that much less suited
to such frivolities.

If you are old, try to look at yourself with the eyes of other
men, to see just how unseemly for you is lechery, which even
in young men ought to be pitied and chastised but in an old
codger is revolting, an object of derision even to its devotees.
Of all monstrosities nothing is more monstrous than senile
lasciviousness. Oh, Dotage, forgetful of yourself! At least
look in the mirror at your white hair, your brow corrugated
with wrinkles, your cadaverous face, and when you have one
foot already in the grave play a game more compatible with
your years! At least, with the admonition—compulsion,
rather!—of age, behave the way you should have from
simply the dictates of reason.

Pleasure herself now rebuffs you: "I am no longer suitable
for you," she says, "nor are you fit company for me. You have
played enough, eaten enough, drunk enough. It is time for
you to go. Why do you keep on pressing for the pleasures of
this life when even life itself will soon forsake you? Now is
the time for that spiritually symbolic concubine Abishag[8] to
begin to rest in your embrace. Let her warm your mind with
holy passion and heat your chilled limbs in her embrace."

THIRTY-FOUR

An Epilogue of Remedies against the Prickings of Lust

Now, TO RECAPITULATE briefly, these are the most effective
ways of rendering yourself immune to carnal snares: first, be
wary and careful to shun the occasion of all of them. This
principle you will also wisely follow in other cases (because
the man who loves danger deserves to perish), but these are

extremely deadly Sirens whom scarcely anyone has escaped except those who kept their distance. Next come regulation of sleep and diet, temperance even in permissible pleasures, being mindful of your own death, and meditating upon the death of Christ.

These practices will also help you: living with chaste and upright people and avoiding like the plague the talk of corrupt and dissolute persons; shunning idle anxiety and slothful leisure, but exercising your mind severely in the contemplation of things celestial and in honorable studies, especially devoting yourself wholeheartedly to the investigation of Holy Scripture and praying often and sincerely, particularly whenever temptation assails you.

THIRTY-FIVE

Against the Provocations to Avarice

IF YOU SEE that either you are naturally rather prone to the vice of avarice or are tempted by Satan, recollect—in accordance with the above rules—the dignity of your condition, who were created and redeemed only for this one thing, that you might always enjoy that highest of all Good. Indeed, God put together the whole fabric of the universe in order that everything might serve your purpose. How squalid, then, and how mean-spirited not to use but to cherish overly things inanimate and commonplace.

Do away with human error and what will gold and silver be except red earth or white? Are you, as a follower of a penniless Christ and one called to a far more valuable possession, going to gape with awe over the importance of stuff every pagan philosopher scorned? Not to have wealth but to rise above it—this is greatness. But the vulgar—Christian only in name—contradict me and rejoice in adroitly deceiving themselves.

"Necessity itself," they say, "encourages us to get property; if we had none we could not even live. If we do not have enough, we live too poorly; but if we are fairly well to do, it affords a lot of advantages. When a man has substantial property he looks after his health, takes care of his children, is useful to his friends, is immune to disfavor and, finally, has a better reputation."

Out of many thousands of Christians you will have trouble finding even one or two who will not say and think such stuff. But let me answer it point by point. First of all, since they disguise their cupidity under the name of necessity, I will counter them with the gospel parable of the lilies and birds which live from day to day, and which Christ urges us to emulate.[1] I will reply to them that He did not permit His disciples to carry even a wallet or a little purse.[2] I will reply that He commanded us to seek first the kingdom of God, and promised that when everything else had been renounced all things would be given to us.[3]

When did He ever fail to supply necessary food to those who have zealously devoted themselves to goodness? How little nature actually requires of us! But you measure necessity, not by the needs of nature, but by the limits of your own greed. To the devout, on the other hand, whatever satisfies nature is enough.

I do not much care, though, for those fellows who in one sweep give up all their own property so that they may the more brazenly beg someone else's.

It is no sin to have money, but being impressed by it is akin to vice. If it pours in upon you, discharge the office of a good steward; but if you are deprived of it do not fret as if you had lost something important but rejoice instead that a perilous responsibility has been removed. Truly, anyone who consumes the best part of life in heaping up wealth, who thinks of that as something wonderful and noteworthy, having a pile that would suffice for a life as long as Nestor's—him you may perhaps call a good business man, but I would certainly not call him a Christian when he is dependent solely upon himself and has no confidence in the promises of Christ. When His goodness benignly feeds and clothes little sparrows,[4] will it—of all things—fail a devout and faithful man?

But let us evaluate even those goods which wealth is supposed to provide. In the first place, even by the consensus of pagan philosophers riches hold last place among useful goods; and according to the categories of Epictetus, everything except virtue of mind is irrelevant to man himself and nothing is so irrelevant or extraneous as money, nothing brings so little advantage.[5] If you owned all the gold or precious stones in the world, would your mind for that reason be worth a hair more? Would it be wiser? Would it be more knowledgeable? Would you be in better shape physically? Younger? Handsomer? More vigorous?

Wealth facilitates the pursuit of pleasures, true, but the ruinous ones. It gets us honor, but in the long run what kind? Obviously it invests us with a counterfeit brand that impresses nobody but fools, and to please fools is virtually a reproach. Real honor means to be praised by the praiseworthy; the highest honor is to have found favor with Christ. True honor is the reward of virtue, not of your money. Suppose the rabble do fawn upon you and esteem you. Stupid, those people are admiring your clothes, not you. Why not look into yourself and observe the wretched poverty of your mind? If the vulgar saw that, it would consider pitiable what it now calls happy.

But money gets us friends, you say? I admit it, but they are false ones. Nor does it get them for you but for itself. In fact, the rich man is in this respect most unhappy, because he cannot even tell who his friends are. One man secretly hates

him for his stinginess; another envies him because he is too
rich; a third, motivated by self-interest, fawns and smiles
upon him in order to get something out of him. The fellow
most ostentatiously affectionate prays for his hasty demise.
No one loves him so much that he would not rather have
him dead than alive. No one is friend enough to let him hear
the truth. And if there is some rare person who deeply loves
a rich man, that rich man can never regard anyone else without suspicion: he judges every person to be a vulture, greed-
ily eyeing a prospective carrion; he thinks all men are flies,
swarming over him for their own feeding. Any advantage,
therefore, that money seems to bring is altogether bogus, a
thing of shadows, an illusion.

It does, however, produce many real evils and take away
a host of real benefits. Accordingly, if you balance the account on debit and credit sides you will assuredly find that
wealth never brings as many advantages as disadvantages.
With what painful efforts are riches won! With what dangers and worry are they held on to! With what grief are they
lost! For this reason Christ calls them thorns,[6] since with a
thousand vexations they lacerate all peace of mind, which
is sweeter to man than anything else. They never satisfy
one's thirst but aggravate it more and more. They drive us
headlong into every crime.

Nor should you vainly gloss over matters to yourself, saying that there is nothing to prevent one from being both rich
and devout. Remember what Truth has spoken: that it is easier for a camel to pass through the eye of a needle than for
a rich man to enter the kingdom of heaven.[7] Clear and unexceptionable is the remark of Jerome: "The rich man is either
the master of iniquity or its heir."[8] Great fortunes are never
accumulated or preserved without sin. Think of how much
more desirable riches they will deprive you, for any lover of
money hates the very nature of virtue, hates all noble practices. Paul, moreover, gives the name of idolatry only to the

sin of covetousness,[9] nor is any other sin whatsoever less compatible with Christ. You cannot serve both God and Mammon.[10]

THIRTY-SIX

An Epilogue of Remedies against the Sin of Avarice

So YOU WILL give up standing in awe of money if you scrupulously distinguish between apparent advantages and real ones; if you will learn to fix the mind's eye upon that Highest Good and love the thing which when present—even if everything else is lacking—abundantly satisfies the heart of man; which is too spacious for any of the good things of this world to fill; if you will repeatedly remind yourself of the condition you were in when the earth first welcomed you at your birth, and the condition it is going to receive you in when you die; if you always keep in mind that fool to whom it was said: "Tonight they require your soul of you, and these things you have laid up, whose will they be?"[1]; if you will turn your mind from the corrupt values of the mass of humanity to the poverty of Mary, the Apostles, the martyrs, and especially of Christ your Head, and always set before you that fearsome word "Woe" with which Christ threatens the rich men of this temporal life.[2]

THIRTY-SEVEN

Against Ambition

IF AMBITION EVER tantalizes your mind with its charms, you
will guard yourself by these means. Following the directions
we have already given, get your teeth into this principle:
that the only true honor proceeds from true virtue and that
even this reputation it is sometimes necessary to avoid, as
Christ Jesus has taught us in word and deed. The sole honor,
therefore, that a Christian must look for is to be approved by
God, not by men; for as the Apostle says, surely the one He
commends has been commended indeed.[1] But when honor is
bestowed on a man for some ignoble action, and that by ignoble people, this is no honor but colossal infamy. If it is
conferred for some irrelevant reason—good looks, for example, or strength, or riches, or family—not even then is it properly called honor; no one deserves honor for that thing which
he cannot take credit for. If it is bestowed for some sterling
quality, it will indeed be honor, but the person who merits
it will not court it. He will be truly satisfied with virtue itself
and a pure conscience.

Note, therefore, how laughable are those glories, inflamed
by which the common run of men pant for so feverishly. In
the first place, who grants them? Obviously those who cannot discriminate between the genuine and the sham. Why
do they grant them? Frequently for invalid reasons, sometimes for base ones. To whom? Those who do not deserve
them. Therefore, whoever tenders an honor does so either
out of fear (in which case he must in turn be feared) or that
you may do him a favor (and then he is mocking you) or because he marvels at bagatelles which deserve no honor (and
in that case he is to be pitied), or because he considers you

blessed with the qualities to which honor is due. If he is mistaken, take care to become the man he thinks you are; but
if he is right, attribute every honor you have to Him you owe
them to, as well as those qualities upon which the honor is
bestowed. It is no more becoming to arrogate honor to yourself than virtue.

In any case, what is more insane than to measure your own
value by the standards of mere men who, whenever it pleases
them, have the power of taking away the very honor they
bestow and of disgracing the one they just now honored?
Surely nothing is more absurd than either being entranced
by such laurels when they come or vexed when they are
taken away. That they are not genuine you should know by
the fact that you share them with the worst thugs. In fact,
they commonly come to no one more abundantly than those
who are least deserving of real esteem.

Consider how happy is the serenity of a life private and
unassuming, removed from every upheaval of pride. On the
other hand, how thorny, how full of cares, perils, and griefs
is the life of great men. How hard it is not to forget oneself
in good fortune. What a problem to keep from falling when
you are standing on a slippery spot! Think how bitter is the
tumble from eminence, how every distinction is coupled
with the heaviest burden, how the stern verdict of the Highest Judge will await those who, while grasping for glory,
have put themselves before everyone else. For certainly
God's mercy will be extended to the person who has humbled himself, as it will be to a little child; but the fellow who
has exalted himself as a paragon has excluded the help of
Grace.[2]

The example of Christ your Chief should always be firmly
fixed in your mind. By worldly standards who was more commonplace, more insignificant, more contemptible? Remember how He who was greater than any honor whatsoever
shunned even those distinctions tendered Him, how He de-

spised honor when He sat on an ass, how He condemned
such things when He was decked out in a robe and crowned
with thorns, how He elected an inglorious death. But the
Father has glorified the One whom the world has scorned.
Let your glory be in the Cross of Christ,[3] in whom is your salvation. Of what use to you are temporal glories if He rejects
you, if God despises you and angels abhor you?

THIRTY-EIGHT

Against Pride and Swelling of the Spirit

You WILL NOT become puffed up if, in the words of that most
widely known maxim, you know yourself; that is, if you
count as a gift from God, not your own doing, anything of
substance or beauty or distinction in you. Conversely, anything base or mean or ugly, this you yourself should take all
responsibility for. If you keep in mind how squalid was your
conception and birth, how naked and defenseless, how ani-
mal-like, how pitiable you were when you crept out into the
light of day, how that puny body of yours is exposed on all
sides to so many ailments, so many accidents and tribulations
—how little it takes shortly to put an end to that gross and
monstrous tumidity of spirit!
    Examine the sort of thing it is that makes you so pleased
with yourself. If it is for routine accomplishments, it is folly;
if it is for dishonorable ones, it is madness; if it is for honorable ones, it is ingratitude. Remember that nothing is more
positive proof of muddleheadedness and stupidity than to be
so pleased with yourself. Moreover, there is no more lamentable kind of folly. If your heart begins to swell because some
trifling fellow servilely defers to you, think how a much
greater and mightier God hovers above your own head, a
God who bends down every arrogant neck and levels every

hill to the plains,[1] who did not even spare the pride of an angel.

And, if you will permit me to speak in a lighter vein, this device will also be useful; always compare yourself with those who excel you. Suppose you are charmed by your own physical endowments; compare yourself to those who surpass you in comeliness. If you preen yourself on your erudition, look at those people who by comparison make you seem a complete ignoramus. You should be conscious, too, not of what distinctive qualities you have but of how much you do not have, and, like Paul, unmindful of what is past, press forward to what lies ahead.[2]

Moreover, it will be no bad policy if, when the tempest of pride is raging, we then convert our very evils into antidotes, driving out one poison with another, so to speak. So it will come about that if either fortune or folly has given us some great physical vice or some notable frailty to sting our hearts, we fix this defect before our eyes and, after the manner of the peacock, scrutinize ourselves most keenly in that area where we are most unlovely. Thus our crests will at once be made to fall.

And beside this, remember that God is more hostile to this sin of pride than to any other, and that among men it is everywhere the object of especial hatred and contempt, while on the other hand modesty wins the favor of God and captures the goodwill of men. In summation, therefore, I should say that two things above all will ward off arrogance: one, keeping in mind just what you are in yourself—repugnant when you enter life, a bubble throughout the course of it, worm's meat when you leave it—and, two, remembering what Christ became for your sake.

THIRTY-NINE

Against Anger and Eagerness for Vengeance

WHEN BURNING GRIEF of heart goads you to vengeance, remember that nothing is more unlike anger than the thing which anger counterfeits,[1] namely, courage. For nothing is so unmanly, so weak, so indicative of a contemptible spirit as taking pleasure in getting even. You want to seem valiant because you do not stand for an injury's going unavenged, but precisely by this very trait you exhibit your childishness, since you lack the control over your passions which is the quality of a man. How much more courageous, how much more large-spirited to overlook someone else's folly than to imitate it!

But he has done you wrong! He is insolent! He is insulting!

Then the more despicable he is, the more careful you should be not to become like him. What devilish madness is it, that in order to pay back someone else's wrongdoing, you yourself become more wicked than he? If you scorn the insult, everyone will know that you did not deserve it, but if you are outraged by it, you have already strengthened the case of the person who insulted you.

Consider, then, the fact as it stands: if you have received any injury, you do not ease it a bit by revenge but only aggravate it. For what will be the eventual result of these reciprocal injuries if everyone hastens to retaliate in kind for his own grievance? Enemies multiply on all sides, the grievance is exacerbated, and the longer it lasts the more incurable it is. But by mildness and forbearance even the man who did the wrong is not infrequently cured, and, doing an about-face, changes from foe to very staunch friend. Through vengeance, however, that very injury which you wish to ward off recoils upon yourself, and not without usurious interest on the capital.

In avoiding wrath you will find it rather helpful to consider—along with the preceding list of precepts—that one man cannot harm another (if the other refuses to be harmed) except in those areas which are only extrinsic goods and do not signify much in terms of the intrinsic man. For God alone is able to deprive you of the valid good things of the mind, something He is not likely to do except to the ungrateful. He alone can bestow gifts, something He is not in the habit of giving to the insolent and cruel. Therefore, no Christian is hurt by anyone but himself; an offense offends no one except the offender.

And these suggestions—though somewhat less cogent—are also helpful in preventing you from nursing any vexation of mind. Mustering together the circumstances of the rhetoricians, make light of your grievance at the same time that you minimize the other fellow's offense in just such a manner as this: "He has done me wrong but it will easily be mended. Moreover, he is a boy, he is ignorant of the world, he is a young man, she is a woman, he acted at somebody else's prompting, he was heedless, he was dead drunk—it is best to overlook the injury." And likewise: "The offense was grave, but he is my father, or my brother, or a teacher, or a friend, or my wife. It is fitting to excuse this injury out of deference to either the love or the respect due that person." Or, by the process of comparison, you may balance this ill turn against the good turns he has done you, or against the injuries you have given him: "To be sure, he has done me a wrong, but at other times how often he has done me good! It is an ungracious spirit to forget good deeds and be mindful only of bad ones. Just now he offends me, but how often has he been offended by me! I should overlook his fault so that, moved by my example, he may overlook mine when I offend."

Finally, a much more effective device will be for you to consider, when some man has inflicted an injury upon you, just what sins, and how great, and how often, you have committed against God, and how many charges He could convict you of. To the extent that you pardon the trespasses of your brother, to that extent God will pardon yours.[2] Himself the Creditor, He has shown us this way of paying our debts, and He will not go back on the law which He himself made. You scurry off to Rome to be absolved of your sins, you sail to Saint James, you buy the most sweeping remissions. Now I do not condemn *what* you do but the fact that it is *all* you do. Once you have sinned, there is no better way of reconciling yourself to God than by reconciling yourself to your brother who has sinned against you. Pardon the trivial offense of your neighbor (and any harm one man does to another is trivial) so that Christ may pardon the countless thousands of your offenses.

"But," you say, "it is hard to keep one's temper from flaring up."

Does it ever occur to you that what Christ endured for your sake was far more difficult? What were you when He was giving His priceless life for your sake? Were you not His enemy? With what clemency He endures you as every day you repeat your same old sins! Finally, with what meekness did He suffer abuse, chains, lashes, and ultimately the most shameful kind of death! Why take pride in the Head if you do not care to be in the Body? You will not be a member of Christ unless you follow in Christ's footsteps.

"But," you say, "the man doesn't deserve to be pardoned."

By the same token did you, whom God pardoned, deserve to be? Do you expect to have mercy for yourself and at the same time apply strict justice to your brother? Is it so much for you, a sinner, to pardon another sinner when Christ prayed to the Father for those who crucified Him?[3] Is it difficult not to strike back at your brother, whom you are commanded to love?[4] Is it difficult not to pay back an injury when, unless you do return a kindness for it, you will not be to your equal what Christ was to His servant?[5] Last of all, if the person to whom you return evil is unworthy, nevertheless you are worthy in doing it; and Christ, for whose sake you do it, is worthy.

"But if I endure one injury, I invite a new one. He will repeat the offense if he gets away with this one."

If you can avoid the injury without offense, avoid it; if you can ease it, ease it; if you can repair it, repair it; if you can heal a lunatic, heal him. But if you cannot, let him perish alone rather than with you. Think of the fellow who supposes that he has done you harm as worthy of pity, not punishment. If you want to be angry in a praiseworthy fashion, be angry with the vice, not the man.

But the more naturally susceptible you are to this fault, the more vigilantly you should guard yourself against it; and once and for all impress this rule upon your mind: never say or do anything while you are angry. Do not trust yourself when you are thus agitated. Be suspicious of whatever an irate mind suggests, even if it is righteous. Remember that between a madman and someone crazed with anger there is no more difference than that existing between chronic and temporary insanity. Control yourself by thinking of how many things deserving of punishment you have said or done in wrath, things you vainly wish could be changed. Then when choler boils up in you, if you cannot wholly defend yourself from it, at least get a grip on yourself sufficiently to realize that you are not in your right mind. Being aware of this is no small step in the direction of sanity!

Think of it this way: "Now, of course, I am strongly provoked to such and such action, but a little later I will feel otherwise. Why should I, in the meantime, angrily say something to a friend which afterward, when I am calmer, I cannot retract? Why should I now do in a rage what I shall be very sorry for when I have recovered? Why, rather, should not reason and piety and Christ bring to pass this thing which a bit later the mere passage of time will effect?" To no one, I suppose, has nature given so much black bile that he cannot control himself at least to this extent.

But it will be best to so condition the mind by education, reason, and habit that you are not upset at all. This will have been achieved if, angered only by the fault, you pay back a charitable action in return for abuse.

To conclude, then, natural moderation should not allow passion totally to rule you. Not to be wrathful at all is most Godlike and, for that reason, most becoming. To overcome evil with good is to emulate the perfect charity of Christ Jesus. To repress anger, to keep a tight rein upon it, is the part of a wise man. To succumb to temper is not even the part of a man, but of mere beasts—and wild ones to boot. If it helps to realize how little it becomes a man to be overcome by anger, sometime when you are calm, look at the face of an enraged person; or when you are enraged, go to a mirror. When your reddened eyes glare like that, when your cheeks turn white, your lips writhe, your mouth slavers, your limbs quiver, your voice howls, your movements go awry—who would look upon you as a man?

You see, dear friend, what a vast amount of time and space would be necessary to treat the rest of the vices in a similar manner. But we will strike our sails in the middle of the trip: what remains will be left to your own discretion. It was not our design, and would be an endless job, to go on as we have thus begun, arguing against every kind of sin— sin by sin—as in an oratorical exercise, and then urging you toward the contrasting virtues. I wished to do only what I believed would be enough for you, to point out some kind of general principles for the inexperienced fighter, by means of which you could defend yourself against the reiterative evils of your former life.

, what we have done in one or two things by
nples, this you must do, not only one by one but
articular regard to those vices which you have
yourself especially susceptible to, either by reason of a natural frailty or a deficiency in training. Against
these specific vices certain rules must be impressed upon
the tablet of the mind and, so that they will not be forgotten
because of lack of practice, continually reviewed: against
the sin of detraction, for example, and obscenity, envy, gluttony, and the like. These things are the only enemies of
Christian soldiers, and against their assault the spirit must
be fortified well ahead by means of prayer, the wisdom of
sages, the teachings of Holy Scripture and especially of
Christ.

Although I have no doubt that the reading of Scripture
would sufficiently provide you with all these resources, nevertheless brotherly love has encouraged me at least to en-
large and stiffen your noble resolution as well as I could
with this offhand little piece. This I have done somewhat
hastily because I was rather afraid you might fall into that
type of superstitious ritualism of the religious who, sometimes with an eye to their own profit, sometimes with limit-
less zeal, but never with adequate knowledge, compass sea
and land, and wherever they stumble across a man con-
valescing from sin into a better life, try immediately, with
outrageous inducements, threats, and blandishments, to steer
him into monastic life, as if there were no Christians outside
of a cowl. Then, when they have filled his heart with gnaw-
ing anxiety and insoluble perplexity, they tie him to certain piddling traditions of human origin, simply push him
into a kind of Judaism, and teach him to be afraid but not to
love.[6]

Monasticism is not piety[7] but a way of living, either useful
or useless in proportion to one's moral and physical disposi-

tion. For my part, I neither urge you into it nor dissuade you from it. This only I suggest: that you not define holiness by what you eat, by ritual, or by any visible object, but by these principles we have been discussing. In whatever things you find the true likeness of Christ, join yourself to these things.

Next, when there are no men around you whose society improves you, withdraw as much as you can from human companionship and converse with the saints, the prophets, the Apostles, and with Christ. Above all, however, make Paul your intimate friend. Him you should always cling to, "meditating upon him day and night"[8] until you commit to memory every word.

For some time now we have been working with great energy on a commentary upon his works, a bold undertaking indeed; nevertheless, relying upon God's help we shall take unremitting pains that we may not seem—after Origen, Ambrose, Augustine, and so many other more recent exegetes— to have undertaken this task without any reason or success whatsoever. And so that certain carpers who think it proof of the deepest piety to know nothing about good literature may understand that even though we have esteemed, ever since our youth, the more cultivated forms of classical learning, and have acquired, not without considerable loss of sleep, a modest understanding of both Greek and Latin, in so doing we did not have an eye on empty fame or puerile gratification of the mind, but had planned far in advance to adorn the Lord's temple, as well as we could, with rare treasures, the temple which some barbarous illiterates have disgraced beyond measure, so that by means of these treasures fine intellects could be kindled into a love for Holy Scripture.

For your sake, however, we have taken a few days away from this very weighty task in order that we might, so to speak, point out the road which leads directly to Christ. I pray, too, that Jesus, the inspiration (as I hope) of such a

purpose, may benignly consent to favor your sound beginning; better yet, that He may increase His grace and make
it perfect in transforming you, so that you may swiftly grow
strong in Him and develop into full manhood. So farewell
in Him, friend and brother, one always dear indeed to my
heart, but now dearer than ever, and more pleasing.

At the town of St. Omer, in the year of Christ's birth, 1501.

Notes

THE following references will be abbreviated in this way throughout the Notes:

Allen. Percy Stafford Allen, Helen May Allen, and Heathcote William Garrod, eds. *Opus Epistolarum Des. Erasmi Roterodami.* Oxford: 1906-1947. 10 vols.

Bailey. N. Bailey, trans., and E. Johnson, ed. *The Colloquies of Desiderius Erasmus Concerning Men, Manners and Things.* London: 1900. 3 vols.

Battles. Ford Lewis Battles. "Erasmus, Enchiridion," in Matthew Spinka, ed., *Advocates of Reform.* Library of Christian Classics. Philadelphia, Pa.: 1953. Vol. XIV.

Dean. Leonard F. Dean, trans. *The Praise of Folly by Desiderius Erasmus.* Chicago, Ill.: 1946.

Enchiridion. All references are, unless otherwise specified, to the present translation, which was made from an octavo edition printed by Jean Knoblock, *Enchiridion Militis Christiani, Saluberrimis praeceptis refertum, authore D. Eras. Roterodamo, cui accessit nova, mireque utilis Praefatio.* Apud Felicem Argentinam. Strasbourg: 1523.

John. All references to John are to the Gospel, the fourth book of the New Testament. All references to I John or II John are to the Epistles.

Opera Omnia. Joannes Clericus. *Erasmi Opera Omnia.* Leiden: 1703-1706.

Packer and Johnston. J. I. Packer and O. R. Johnston, trans., *Martin Luther On the Bondage of the Will.* London: 1957.

INTRODUCTION

1. In Roland H. Bainton, *The Reformation of the Sixteenth Century* (Boston, Mass.: 1952), 82-83.

2. See F. van der Haeghen, ed., *Bibliotheca Erasmiana*, I (Ghent: 1903-1907), 79-84.

3. See Preserved Smith, *Erasmus* (New York and London: 1923), 158.

4. *Enchiridion*, 198. The passage was censured in Madrid in 1584. Cf. Battles, 378 n.

5. Cf. M. Bataillon, *Érasme et l'Espagne* (Paris: 1937), 220-221.

6. In Allen, I, 1.

7. The opening and closing passages, presumably the vestigial traces of the original letter, are reprinted in Allen, I, 164. One is reminded of the conventionality of the opening sentences by a comparison with Jerome's letter to Heliodorus on the ascetic life (XIV.), and to Nepotian on a clergyman's duties (LII), which contain definite parallels in phrasing. Erasmus was a great admirer of Jerome.

8. Allen, III, 698.

9. Allen, III, 858.

10. Allen, I, 181.

11. Allen, II, 421.

12. Cf. Allen, IV, 439.

13. *Erasmus*, 321-322.

14. *A History of Political Thought in the Sixteenth Century* (New York: 1960), 3.

15. Allen, VI, 1537.

16. Quoted in Heinrich Boehmer, *The Road to Reformation*, trans. by J. W. Doberstein and Theodore G. Tappet (New York: 1957), 160.

17. From his Table Talk, quoted in J. J. Mangan, *Life, Character, and Influence of Desiderius Erasmus* (New York: 1927), 255.

18. *Enchiridion*, 82.

19. *The Reformation of the Sixteenth Century*, 69.

20. *Enchiridion*, 155.

21. *Enchiridion*, 163.

22. *Enchiridion*, 193.

23. See Craig R. Thompson, trans., *Ten Colloquies of Erasmus* (New York: 1957), 158.

24. *De Servo Arbitrio*. See Packer and Johnston, 251-252.

25. Packer and Johnston, 103-104.

26. "On the Dignity of Man," in Ernst Cassirer, Paul Oskar Kristellar, and John Herman Randall, Jr., eds., *The Renaissance Philosophy of Man* (University of Chicago Press: 1948), 229.

27. "Concerning the Mind," in Cassirer, Kristellar, and Randall, Jr., eds., *The Renaissance Philosophy of Man*, 204.

28. Packer and Johnston, 43.

29. *Enchiridion*, 192.

30. Packer and Johnston, 43.

31. Packer and Johnston, 19.

32. Packer and Johnston, 60.

33. *Erasmus*, 351.

34. Quoted in P. S. Allen, *Erasmus: Lectures and Wayfaring Sketches* (Oxford: 1934), 90.

35. Allen, III, 358.

36. See, for example, Craig R. Thompson, trans. and ed., *Inquisitio de Fide* (Yale University Press: 1950), a colloquy dealing obviously with the Lutheran "heresy."

37. *The Reformation of the Sixteenth Century*, 69.

38. Packer and Johnston, 36.

39. Packer and Johnston, 92.

40. *Enchiridion*, 131, 135.

41. Cf. Packer and Johnston, 60.

42. Johan Huizinga, *Erasmus and the Age of Reformation* (New York: 1957), 147.

TWO: IN THIS LIFE ONE MUST BE ON GUARD

1. Job 7: 1 (Vulgate). The King James version is less military in imagery.

2. In Greek mythology the arrows of Hercules figured in the help he gave the Olympian gods in their war with the Giants, as well as in the sixth of his labors, the shooting of the Stymphalian birds. On his death he gave his bow and arrows to Philoctetes,

who made them famous at the siege of Troy. Cephalus accidentally killed his wife, Procris, while hunting with a javelin which she herself had given him and which could not miss its mark.

3. Cf. John 15: 18-19 and 17: 14.

4. Cf. Vergil's *Aeneid*, V. 84.

5. *cuticulam (ut aiunt) curamus otiosi.* In the *Adagia* (*Opera Omnia*, II, 546E), Erasmus cites the phrase *Cuticulam curare* as one used by Horace and other classical writers to describe people more intent upon pleasure than fame: *Nam qui voluptati student magis quam famae, unum hoc curant, ut cutis summa niteat. . . .*

6. Jeremiah 6: 14; 8: 11.

7. Isaiah 48: 22.

8. Cf. II Corinthians 6: 14.

9. I Peter 1: 18-19.

10. Matthew 12: 30; Luke 11: 23.

11. Romans 6: 23.

12. Cf. *Iliad*, XXIII. 260 and *Aeneid*, V. 110.

13. I Corinthians 2: 9.

14. Cf. *Iliad*, XXII. 395 ff.

15. Luke 4: 4.

16. Cf. I John 4: 7-8.

17. Cf. I Corinthians 12: 26.

18. Matthew 23: 27.

19. Cf. Psalms 5: 9.

20. I Corinthians 3: 17 and 6: 19.

21. Cf. Matthew 12: 34-35.

22. John 6: 68.

23. Romans 8: 31.

24. I Peter 2: 22; I John 3: 5.

25. John 16: 33.

THREE: CONCERNING THE WEAPONS OF CHRISTIAN SOLDIERING

1. Nations living in Canaan, the land promised to the Hebrews. Cf. Deuteronomy 7: 1 ff.

2. Thessalonians 5: 17.

3. Horace, *Ars Poetica*, 410-411.

4. James 1: 6.

5. The disciples James and John were sons of Zebedee. Cf. Matthew 20: 22 and Mark 11: 35-38.

6. Exodus 17: 11-12.

7. Matthew 6: 7-8.

8. I Corinthians 14: 19.

9. Exodus 14: 15.

10. Psalms 121: 1.

11. Cf. Exodus 17: 5-7.

12. Psalms 22: 5 (Vulgate), which has *qui tribulant nos.* Cf. 23: 5 in the King James version.

13. II Timothy 3: 16.

14. Exodus 16: 14.

15. John 6: 60.

16. Exodus 16: 15.

17. Psalms 22: 2 (Vulgate), which reads *Super aquam refectionis educavit me.*

18. Erasmus seems to be paraphrasing Ecclesiasticus 24: 40-41: *Ego sapientia effudi flumina. Ego quasi trames aquae immensae de fluvio ego quasi fluvii Dioryx, & sicut aquaductus exivi de paradiso.*

19. Ezekiel 47: 1-6.

20. Genesis 26: 18.

21. Exodus 15: 27.

22. John 4: 6.

23. John 9: 1-17.

24. John 13: 5.

25. Cf. Joshua 1: 8.

26. *Ad Adulescentes: Sermones de Legendis Libris Gentilium,* in Migne, *Patrologia Graeca,* XXXI, 563-590.

27. *De Ordine,* I, 8, 23-24.

28. Epistle LXX, 2.

29. Cf. *De Doctrina Christiana,* II, 40-61.

30. Exodus 18: 13-27.

31. Epistle LIII, 7.

32. Titus 1: 15.

33. Song of Solomon 6: 8.

34. Deuteronomy 21: 12.

35. Hosea 1: 2-11.

36. Exodus 12: 34-39.

37. Exodus 16: 20.

38. I Chronicles 13: 10; II Samuel 6: 6-7.

39. Romans 7: 14.

40. Not the first expression of Erasmus' distaste for what, in a letter to Colet two years earlier, he had called "this new breed of divines" who grow old in sophistical hairsplitting (Allen, I, 108). Writing to Thomas Grey in 1497, he contemptuously dismissed them as pseudo-theologians, and a catalogue of their shortcomings provoked him to some of his choicest invective: . . . *quorum cerebellis nihil putidius, lingua nihil barbarius, ingenio nihil stupidius, doctrina nihil spinosius, moribus nihil asperius, vita nihil fucatius, oratione nihil virulentius, pectore nihil nigrius* (Allen, I, 64).

41. Cf. I Corinthians 3: 1-2. Erasmus liked this image. See, for example, *Paraclesis* (*Opera Omnia*, V, 140).

42. John 6: 63.

43. II Corinthians 3: 6.

44. Romans 7: 14.

45. I Corinthians 2: 13.

46. John 4: 20 ff.

47. I Corinthians 12: 31; 14: 2 ff.

48. Colossians 2: 16; Romans 14: 3.

49. Revelation 3: 7 and 5: 1.

50. *Iliad*, XVIII, 478 ff.

51. Perhaps a reference to the "tower of David builded for an armoury." Cf. Song of Solomon 4: 4 and II Samuel 22: *passim*.

52. Horace, *Carmina*, III, 3: 7-8.

53. I Samuel 17: 38-40 (I Kings in the Vulgate).

54. Cf. I Samuel 17: 40 and I Corinthians 14: 19.

55. Cf. Matthew 4: 1-11.

56. Wisdom of Solomon 5: 18-21.

57. 59: 17.

58. II Corinthians 10: 4-5.

59. Cf. Ephesians 6: 13-17 and II Corinthians 6: 17.

60. Romans 8: 35-39.

61. I Corinthians 4: 13.

FOUR: THE FIRST POINT OF WISDOM IS TO KNOW YOURSELF; CONCERNING TWO KINDS OF WISDOM: SEEMING AND REAL

1. Cf. John 14: 27.

2. Wisdom of Solomon 7: 30.

3. I Corinthians 1: 30.

4. I Corinthians 1: 23-24.

5. I Corinthians 3: 18-19.

6. I Corinthians 1: 19-20.

7. Cf. Matthew 15: 14.

8. Romans 16: 19.

9. *Works and Days,* 296-297.

10. Psalms 2: 4.

11. Wisdom of Solomon 4: 18.

12. Wisdom of Solomon 5: 3-4; Proverbs 1: 26.

13. Cf. James 3: 15 and Philippians 3: 19.

14. Wisdom of Solomon 7: 11-12.

15. Cf. Judith 9: 16.

16. James 1: 5-6.

17. Cf. Proverbs 2: 4-5.

18. Cf. Juvenal, *Satires,* XI. 27.

19. Song of Solomon 1: 7. Erasmus has *pulchra* rather than the scriptural *pulcherrima.*

20. II Corinthians 12: 2.

21. In Greek mythology both Cadmus and Jason had to fight armed men who sprang up from the earth after the heroes had sown dragons' teeth.

22. Joshua 5: 13-14.

FIVE: CONCERNING THE INNER AND OUTER MAN

1. In a letter to Martin Lipsius, Erasmus notes that Edward Lee had attacked this passage for seeming to suggest that the human soul was a part of the divine nature. (See Allen, III, 843, 329.)

2. The proverb *Auribus lupum teneo* appears in the *Adagia* (*Opera Omnia,* II, 190F). Cf. also Terence's *Phormio,* III. 507.

3. Ovid, *Amores,* III. 11, 39. Interestingly enough, in the

exegesis of the proverb above, Erasmus includes the same quotation from Ovid: *Nec tecum possum vivere, nec sine te.* A marginal gloss of 1523 wrongly cites Catullus.

4. In one of the creation stories of Greek mythology, the gods delegated the task of making man to Prometheus and his brother Epimetheus. Cf. Ovid, *Metamorphoses*, I. 2, and Hesiod, *Theogony*, 211-232.

5. See 69B and 42B-45B for the extended passage digested here.

6. Cf. *Iliad*, VIII. 247.

SIX: CONCERNING THE VARIETY OF PASSIONS

1. *Phaedo*, 9B-12E; 64A.

2. *Phaedrus*, 25B-C; 246A ff; 9B-12E.

3. Erasmus alludes, of course, to a commonplace of Renaissance physiology and psychology, the four "humours" or moistures: blood, phlegm, choler, and black bile. An exact balance of these humours made the properly constituted man.

4. Cf. Jeremiah 1: 18 and 15: 20.

5. The remark, which seems to be proverbial, is found in the *Republic*, IV, 435C, as well as in the *Hippias Major*, 304E.

6. Epistle CXXV, *Ad Rusticum Monachum*. Rusticus had entered a monastery on Jerome's advice.

7. *Works and Days*, 290-293.

SEVEN: CONCERNING THE INNER AND OUTER MAN AND THE TWO ASPECTS OF MAN ACCORDING TO HOLY SCRIPTURE

1. Cf. Ephesians 2: 14 and Matthew 10: 34 ff.

2. Galatians 5: 16-17.

3. Romans 8: 13.

4. I Corinthians 9: 27.

5. Galatians 5: 18.

6. Romans 8: 15.

7. Romans 7: 23.

8. II Corinthians 4: 16.

9. I Corinthians 15: 45-50.

10. Romans 7: 24.

11. Galatians 6: 8.
12. Genesis 25: 22-27 and 27: 1-27.
13. Genesis 25: 23 and 27: 40.
14. Cf. Ephesians 5: 22.
15. Ecclesiasticus 42: 14.
16. Genesis 3: 14-15.
17. Genesis 18: 12, 21: 1-5 and 10-12.
18. II Corinthians 12: 7-9.
19. II Corinthians 4: 7.
20. Cf. Vergil, *Georgics,* I. 145-146.
21. *Georgics,* IV. 440-442.
22. *Georgics,* IV. 406-409.
23. *Georgics,* IV. 411-412.
24. Cf. Genesis 32: 24-26.
25. Cf. I Kings 18: 21.
26. Genesis 33: 25-32.
27. Galatians 5: 24.
28. I Kings 19: 11-12.
29. Genesis 32: 30.
30. I Corinthians 1: 29.

EIGHT: CONCERNING THE THREE PARTS OF MAN: SPIRIT, SOUL, AND FLESH

1. Commentary on the Epistle to the Romans, 1: 5; 10.
2. I Thessalonians 5: 23.
3. Isaiah 26: 9.
4. Daniel 3: 86 (Vulgate).
5. I Corinthians 6: 16-17.
6. Proverbs 2: 16-19.
7. Proverbs 6: 24-26. Verse 26 of the Vulgate has *Pretium enim scorti vix unius est panis;* the King James version, "For by means of a whorish woman a man is brought to a piece of bread," effects a considerable shift in the economics of the situation. Erasmus' memory seems to have faltered, however, in the use of *rapit* in the next clause: the Vulgate has *capit.*
8. Proverbs 9: 13-18.
9. *Visne pinquiore, quod aiunt, Minerva tanquam digito tibi*

demonstrari. . . . In the *Adagia* (*Opera Omnia*, II, 42A), Erasmus quotes and explains this proverbial idiom of a thick-witted, doltish Minerva.

10. Cf. I Corinthians 6: 16.

11. Cf. Romans 14: 3.

NINE: CERTAIN GENERAL RULES FOR THE TRUE CHRISTIAN LIFE

1. Job 21: 14.

2. Luke 9: 62.

3. Cf. Psalms 19: 5.

4. Philippians 3: 13.

5. James 1: 12.

TEN: AGAINST THE SIN OF IGNORANCE: THE FIRST RULE (FAITH)

1. James 2: 19.

ELEVEN: THE SECOND RULE (ACTION)

1. Cf. Matthew 11: 12.

2. Cf. Exodus 16: 3.

3. Genesis 19: 17-26.

4. Jeremiah 51: 6. Cf. Isaiah 48: 20.

5. Luke 12: 20.

6. A modification of Psalms 54: 23 (Vulgate). Erasmus has *Iacta cogitatum tuum in Dominum;* the Vulgate has *Iacta super Dominum curam tuam.*

7. Psalms.

8. Matthew 6: 24; II Corinthians 6: 15.

9. Cf. I Kings 18: 21.

10. Revelation 3: 12; 5: 9.

11. Cf. Matthew 7: 13-14.

12. Cf. *Adagia* (*Opera Omnia*, II, 595E ff.)

13. Galatians 6: 14.

14. Matthew 10: 38; 16: 24.

15. Horace, *Carmina*, II, xiv. 12.

TWELVE: THE THIRD RULE (DESPITE ILLUSIONS; CHOOSE THE WAY OF CHRIST)

1. *Aeneid*, VI. 282-295.

2. Horace, *Epistles,* I, 1. 36.

3. Wisdom of Solomon 5: 7.

4. Matthew 11: 29-30.

5. Galatians 6: 7.

6. Matthew 6: 19.

7. Luke 12: 31.

8. Cf. I Kings 8: 20.

9. Cf. Romans 8: 28.

THIRTEEN: THE FOURTH RULE (CHRIST AS THE ONLY GOAL)

1. Matthew 6: 22.

2. I Thessalonians 5: 10. Erasmus elaborates upon the passage.

3. Cf. Matthew 6: 23.

4. A Cynic philosopher of the latter part of the fourth century B.C. He is said to have sacrificed his fortune in accordance with his principles, one story being that he directed his banker to give the money to his sons if they should prove fools, but to the poor if his sons should become philosophers.

5. Prometheus warned his brother Epimetheus against accepting from Zeus the gift of Pandora and her box of evils. Cf. Hesiod, *Works and Days,* 42-105; *Theogony,* 465-616.

6. I Corinthians 7 : 29-31.

7. Cf. I Corinthians 1: 21, 25.

8. A favorite target of Erasmus. Part of his distaste for fasting and vigils seems to have stemmed from his own physical incapacities. He confessed to Bostius, a Carmelite monk, that even at his best he was constitutionally unfit for such practices (Allen, I, 75). Whatever the source of his distaste, however, it came to be a part of a broad attack on those of the clergy who identified holiness with Judaic ceremonialism in garb and fasting. See, for example: his letter to Paul Volz, in Allen, III, 858.

9. The passage beginning here and continuing for three paragraphs was included in the *Index expurgatorius* published at Antwerp in 1571. (See Battles, 331 n.)

10. Saint Christopher, the patron of ferrymen, was martyred about 250 A.D. Although little authentic is known about him, the best-known story concerns his carrying passengers on his back

over a bridgeless river and finding that one of his passengers was God in the person of a little child.

Roch was especially invoked against plague. Legend had it that when he was expelled from the city and driven into the forest to starve, he was fed by dogs. He died in 1327.

Barbara was a virgin martyr of the third century, said to have been beheaded by her father for accepting Christianity.

Apollonia, another virgin martyr of the third century, was invoked against toothache, presumably because her teeth were said to have been knocked out by heathen mobs of Alexandria.

A misguided reverence for saints was, of course, another of Erasmus' favorite butts of ridicule. See, for example: the colloquies "A Pilgrimage For Religion's Sake" and "On the Eating of Fish." The latter contains a passage which rather closely parallels the one above, including the use of most of the same saints. (See Bailey, II, 310 ff; also Dean, 79 ff.)

11. I Timothy 6: 5.
12. Romans 16: 18.
13. Romans 14: 8.
14. I Philippians 1: 23.
15. I Corinthians 12: 31.

FOURTEEN: THE FIFTH RULE (FROM THE VISIBLE TO THE INVISIBLE; THE WAY TO A PURE AND SPIRITUAL LIFE)

1. II Corinthians 4: 6.
2. Malachi 4: 2.
3. *Phaedo*, 80-81; 64A ff.
4. Matthew 10: 38; Luke 14: 27.
5. E.g., Romans 6: 2-12; II Timothy 2: 11.
6. Psalms 44: 22.
7. Colossians 3: 1-2.
8. Matthew 25: 41.
9. In the *Symposium*, 215-217, Alcibiades compares Socrates to statuettes of Silenus, the fat and ugly leader of satyrs who attended Bacchus in his revels. When opened, the statuettes were found to contain the images of the gods. Cf. *Adagia (Opera Omnia*, II, 770D).
10. Cf. Genesis 2: 7-22; 3: 5-24.

11. Progeny of the union between Earth and Tartarus in one of the creation myths, they assaulted heaven and the Olympians with rocks and firebrands and were defeated when Hercules came to the aid of the gods. Cf. Ovid, *Metamorphoses,* I. 150 ff; Appollodorus, I, vi. 1-2.

12. Cf. *Odyssey,* X. 283 ff.

13. Cf. Genesis 25 and 27.

14. I Samuel 17: 49.

15. Judges 16: 19.

16. II Samuel 11: 2-27.

17. Genesis 19: 30, 36.

18. The so-called "Pseudo-Areopagite," who attached the name of the original, named in Acts 17: 34, to certain of his own theological writings, including the one "Concerning Divine Names." He is presumed to have lived sometime during the fourth or fifth centuries.

19. In his *Ratio Verae Theologiae* (*Opera Omnia,* V, 82 ff), Erasmus compares the older theology of Origen, Basil, and Jerome with that of the "modern" scholastics. The earlier was like a golden river; the other, a meager little rivulet and not very pure at that. The scholastics, with their incessant classification and division, only *seemed* learned because men had been conditioned from childhood to learn nothing until it had been mangled and partitioned in this fashion.

20. *City of God,* VIIIC: 5.

21. Cf. II Corinthians 3: 16.

22. II Corinthians 3: 13 ff; I Corinthians 13: 12.

23. John 6: 63.

24. E.g. Romans 8: 12-13.

25. Luke 14: 5; Matthew 12: 11.

26. Mark 8: 22-26.

27. Luke 6: 1-4.

28. Mark 7: 19; Matthew 15: 20.

29. Matthew 9: 10-13.

30. Luke 18: 10-14.

31. Romans 9: 3-5.

32. Matthew 3: 9.

33. Matthew 23: 5. Meaning "safeguard," the phylactery was

a small cubical case containing strips of parchment on which were written summaries of the moral law. The Hebrews bound these phylacteries on the foreheads and right hands when they were at prayer.

34. John 4: 21-24.

35. John 2: 1-10.

36. John 6: 64.

37. Cf. II Esdra 5: 13 (Vulgate).

38. Cf. Romans 6: 4.

39. Cf. the colloquy "On the Eating of Fish" (Bailey, II, 310 ff).

40. Reading *mutum et mortuum,* as in *Opera Omnia,* V, 31E, rather than the *mutum et mutuum* of the 1523 text.

41. Mark 16: 14.

42. John 16: 7.

43. II Corinthians 5: 16.

44. I Corinthians 3: 1. Again, cf. "On the Eating of Fish" (Bailey, II, 259).

45. The material from this point on to the end of Rule Five was included in the *Index expurgatorius* of Antwerp, 1571. (See Battles, 339 n.)

46. Matthew 5: 13.

47. Early Christian hermit, reputed founder of monastic life. Cf. Dean, 107.

48. See Terence, *The Brothers,* I. 99-100.

49. Cf. Matthew 6: 1 ff.

50. Galatians 5: 22-23.

51. Luke 18: 11-12.

52. Romans 8: 1-8.

53. Cf. *Adagia* (*Opera Omnia,* II, 217D).

54. Colossians 2: 18-23; 3: 1-15.

55. Galatians 5: 17-26.

56. Matthew 7: 16.

57. Livy, XXI, iv. 1.

58. Galatians 5: 1.

59. Galatians 3: 24-26.

60. Galatians 4: 3-7.

61. Galatians 5: 13-15.

62. Romans 8: 15. Erasmus misquotes, however. His *Non enim accepistis spiritum adoptionis* does not tally with the Vulgate's *Non enim accepistis spiritum servitutis . . . sed accepistis spiritum adoptionis filiorum.*

63. I Timothy 4: 7-8.

64. II Corinthians 3: 17.

65. John 13: 34-35; 15: 12-13.

66. I Corinthians 13: 1-2.

67. Isaiah 1: 11-15.

68. Isaiah 58: 1-5.

69. Isaiah 1:16 (Vulgate). *Cogitationum* rather than the King James "doings."

70. Isaiah 11: 3.

71. Matthew 25: 1-12.

72. Matthew 7: 21.

73. Isaiah 1: 17.

74. Isaiah 58: 6-7.

75. I Corinthians 8: 11.

76. John 4: 24.

77. *Catonis Disticha,* I. 1. The "distichs" or moralizing couplets of an author who was really unknown; writing, presumably in the second or third century, he came to be called Cato because that name was apparently synonymous with practical wisdom. Erasmus, among many others, brought out an edition of the verses.

78. Psalms 34: 18.

79. Reading *quod requirunt oculi dei,* as in *Opera Omnia,* V, 37D, rather than *reliquerunt,* as in the 1523 text.

80. Ezekiel 8: 7-9.

81. Jeremiah 13: 17.

82. E.g. Matthew 13: 13; Mark 8: 18; and Luke 8: 10.

83. Jeremiah 5: 21.

84. Psalms 45: 13-14.

85. Luke 7: 47.

86. Ezekiel 37: 1-14.

87. Cf. I Samuel 2: 3.

88. Isaiah 59: 4.

89. Romans 10: 2.

90. Isaiah 5: 13.

91. John 6: 9-13.

92. Exodus 17: 6.

93. John 7: 38.

94. *Phaedrus,* 245D-248.

95. Genesis 28: 12.

96. James 4: 8.

97. I Timothy 6: 16.

FIFTEEN: THE SIXTH RULE (DO NOT FOLLOW POPULAR OPINION
BUT ONLY CHRIST)

1. Cf., 484C ff; 506A; 519C. See also *Laws,* II, 659D-662.

2. I.e. Marcus Fabius Quintilian. See *Institutio Oratoria,* I,
viii. 4.

3. Cf. *Protagoras,* 354-358D. For Aristotle's objections, see
Nichomachean Ethics, 1144b and 1145b.

4. Cf. Cicero, *De Oratore,* III, 213.

5. *Republic,* VII, 514A-517B.

6. Luke 12: 32.

7. Matthew 7: 14.

8. Cf. James 2: 14.

9. *Epistles,* I, vi. 37.

10. *Satires,* II, v. 8.

11. *Epistles,* I, i. 53.

12. Cf. Seneca, *Epistulae Morales,* CXV, 14-16.

13. *Confessions,* IV, ii and IX, i.

14. Cf. *Adagia (Opera Omnia,* II, 198F).

15. Cf. Romans 12: 5.

16. Psalms 84: 10.

17. Cf. I Corinthians 1: 27-28.

18. John 8: 39-44.

19. Romans 9: 6-7 (Vulgate). The quotation is not exact, however.

20. Matthew 7: 21.

21. John 8: 44.

22. Galatians 6 : 17.

23. Matthew 13: 46.

24. Ecclesiasticus 1: 26.

25. Revelation 3: 18.

26. Matthew 13: 7.

27. Romans 13: 14.

28. The story alluded to here may be found in Sophocles' *Ajax;* it is not included in the *Iliad.* According to this later version, Ajax was so enraged at losing to Odysseus in the competition for the armor of Achilles that he went mad. With demented laughter he began slaughtering the flocks of sheep in the camp, under the impression that they were his enemies. On coming to his senses, he killed himself.

29. The natives of Miletus, a once-powerful Greek city in Asia Minor, seem to have been proverbial examples of effeminacy and voluptuousness. Cf. *Adagia* (*Opera Omnia*, II, 351F and 352D).

30. In the colloquy "The Epicurean," Erasmus dilates upon the same theme: " . . . don't think that any Lucullus sups more pleasantly upon his Partridges, Pheasants, Turtle-Doves, Hares, Giltheads, Sturgeons, or Lampreys, than a godly Man does upon brown Bread, a Sallad, or Pulse, and Water, or Small-Beer, or a little Wine mixed with a great Deal of Water, because he receives them as sent from a kind Father" (Bailey, III, 259).

31. Hosea 4: 14.

32. Psalms 89: 32-33.

33. Cf. Plato's *Gorgias,* 508E.

34. Philippians 4: 13.

35. John 8: 44.

36. Luke 12; 20.

37. *E.g.: Metamorphoses,* VII. 149-151.

38. Terence, *The Brothers,* II, ii. 216.

39. Isaiah 5: 20.

40. Romans 12: 2.

SIXTEEN: OPINIONS WORTHY OF A CHRISTIAN

1. Cf. Romans 5: 10.

2. Romans 12: 15.

3. Romans 8: 16-17.

4. Ephesians 4: 4-6.

5. Galatians 3: 28.

6. Ephesians 4: 25; 4: 16.

7. I Corinthians 11: 3.

8. I Corinthians 12: 26.

9. In the *Adagia* (*Opera Omnia*, II, 78E), Erasmus cites *Pares cum paribus facillime congregantur*. But *Dissimilitudo mater odii* does not appear, although *Similitudo mater est benevolentiae* does. (The following passage is paralleled in Dean, 102.)

10. Romans 12: 5, Ephesians 4: 4.

11. I Corinthians 12: 12-27. .

12. Romans 12: 4-6.

13. Ephesians 4: 15-16.

14. Galatians 6: 2; Ephesians 4: 25.

15. Matthew 5: 39-45.

16. Matthew 5: 46.

17. Cf. Romans 12: 14 and 17-21.

18. Cf. Matthew 20: 26-28.

19. Cf. Luke 12: 48.

20. This and the two preceding sentences were included in the Antwerp *Index expurgatorius* (Battles, 361 n).

21. Republic, I, 347C.

22. Cf. John 18: 36.

23. Matthew 20: 25-28.

24. Matthew 23: 10.

25. Cf. I John 5: 19.

26. Cf. II Corinthians 2: 17; II Timothy 4: 3-4; Titus I: 10-16.

27. Romans 13: 1.

28. *Protinus surgunt cristae:* a phrase from Juvenal, *Satires*, IV. 70.

29. Luke 16: 2.

30. Luke 3: 11; Matthew 10: 10.

31. II Samuel 11.

32. Genesis 13: 2.

33. I Kings 11: 3.

34. Genesis 9: 21.

35. Genesis 19: 30-36.

36. Luke 7: 37-39.

37. Cf. Galatians 1: 13; I Corinthians 15: 9.
38. Luke 22: 54-62; Matthew 26: 69-75.
38. Genesis 22: 1-10.
40. Matthew 9: 9-10.
41. *Confessions,* IVc, 2; VIc, 15.
42. Cf. I Corinthians 1: 21.
43. Cf. I Corinthians 9: 22.

SEVENTEEN: THE SEVENTH RULE (TRAINING IN THE PRACTICE OF VIRTUE)

1. Quintilian, *Institutio Oratoria,* I, ix. 13 and XII, xi. 30.

EIGHTEEN: THE EIGHTH RULE (THE VALUE OF TEMPTATION)

1. Cf. Hebrews 12: 6.
2. II Corinthians 12: 2-7.
3. I Corinthians 10: 13.

NINETEEN: THE NINTH RULE (VIGILANCE AGAINST SIN)

1. I Peter 5: 8.
2. Cf. Genesis 3: 15.
3. Cf. Psalms 137: 9.

TWENTY-ONE: THE ELEVENTH RULE (TRUST NOT YOURSELF BUT CHRIST)

1. Psalms 90: 5-6 (Vulgate).
2. Philippians 4: 13.
3. John 16: 33.
4. I Corinthians 4: 7.

TWENTY-THREE: THE THIRTEENTH RULE (HAVE HOPE IN FINAL VICTORY BUT BE EVER ON GUARD)

1. Against Celsus, VIII. 44. Cf. Migne, *Patrologia Graeca,* XI, 1581 ff.

2. Habakkuk 2: 1; Isaiah 21: 8.

TWENTY-FOUR: THE FOURTEENTH RULE (TAKE NO VICE LIGHTLY)

1. *Works and Days,* 287-288.

TWENTY-SIX: THE SIXTEENTH RULE (MEET DEFEAT WITH RENEWED EFFORT)

1. See Gellius, *Attic Nights,* XVII, xxi. 31. Cf. *Adagia* (*Opera Omnia,* II, 379D).

TWENTY-SEVEN: THE SEVENTEENTH RULE (THE MYSTERY OF THE CROSS)

1. Cf. I Corinthians 3: 2.
2. Cf. Song of Solomon 7: 8.
3. Romans 8: 9.
4. Isaiah 53: 7.
5. Matthew 8: 20; II Corinthians 8: 9.

TWENTY-EIGHT: THE EIGHTEENTH RULE (THE NOBILITY OF MAN)

1. Cf. I Corinthians 3: 16; 6: 19.

TWENTY-NINE: THE NINETEENTH RULE (BETWEEN GOD AND SATAN)

1. Cf. Galatians 4: 7; John 15: 14.
2. II Peter 2: 19; John 8: 34.

THIRTY: THE TWENTIETH RULE (BETWEEN VIRTUE AND SIN)

1. Matthew 19:29.
2. I Corinthians 2: 9; Isaiah 64: 4.
3. Isaiah 66: 24; Mark 9: 44.
4. Luke 16: 19-24. The passage beginning "while in the meantime the worm of the wicked does not die" and continuing to the end of the paragraph was included in the Antwerp *Index* (Battles, 370 n). It had been under fire long before, however; in a letter to Beda in 1525, Erasmus mentions attacks in Spain, especially on the part of Dominicans, against this passage "in which I seem to deny the fire of Purgatory" (Allen, VI, 1581.)

THIRTY-TWO: THE TWENTY-SECOND RULE (IMPENITENCE THE WORST OF SINS)

1. *Cf.* Isaiah 5: 18.
2. Vergil, *Aeneid,* VI. 128.

3. A fox, having fallen into a well, persuaded a goat to jump in by telling her a drought was coming and it was wise to have water handy. When the goat had leaped in, the fox made his escape by climbing up on her back and horns.

THIRTY-THREE: REMEDIES FOR SOME SPECIFIC SINS AND, FIRST OF ALL, FOR LUST

1. Cf. Wisdom of Solomon 2: 2-5. *Cf.: Adagia (Opera Omnia,* II, 500A ff).

2. Cf. Matthew 25: 41.

3. *Symposium,* 180D-E.

4. Cf. Psalms 91: 11; Proverbs 44: 12.

5. Daniel 3: 55 (Vulgate).

6. Cf. I Corinthians 6: 15-16. A similar passage occurs in the colloquy "On the Eating of Fish" (Bailey, II, 297): "How many Priests are there, that would die before they would participate the Sacrament in a Chalice and Charger, that has not been consecrated by a Bishop, or in their every-Day Clothes? But among them all that are thus nice, how many do we see that are not at all afraid to come to the Lord's Table drunk with the last Night's Debauch?"

7. *Cf.* Ephesians 5: 22-33.

8. I Kings 1: 1-14. Abishag, meaning "Ignorance of the Father," was a girl David introduced into his harem in his old age, hence not for sexual intimacy.

THIRTY-FIVE: AGAINST THE PROVOCATIONS TO AVARICE

1. Matthew 6: 28; Luke 12: 27.

2. Matthew 10: 9-10; Luke 10: 4.

3. Matthew 6: 33; Luke 12: 31.

4. Matthew 10: 29.

5. Cf. Epictetus, *Dissertations,* I, i; III, xxiv. 3, 67 ff.

6. Matthew 13: 22.

7. Matthew 19: 24; Mark 10: 25; Luke 18: 25.

8. Jerome, *Epistles,* 120, 1. Erasmus includes the remark in the *Adagia (Opera Omnia,* II, 351A).

9. Colossians 3: 5: Ephesians 5: 5.

10. Matthew 6: 24.

THIRTY-SIX: AN EPILOGUE OF REMEDIES AGAINST THE SIN OF AVARICE

1. Luke 12: 20 (Vulgate).
2. Luke 6: 24.

THIRTY-SEVEN: AGAINST AMBITION

1. II Corinthians 10: 18.
2. Cf. Luke 14: 11.
3. Galatians 6: 14.

THIRTY-EIGHT: AGAINST PRIDE AND SWELLING OF THE SPIRIT

1. Isaiah 40: 4.
2. Philippians 3: 13.

THIRTY-NINE: AGAINST ANGER AND EAGERNESS FOR VENGEANCE

1. Cf. Juvenal, *Satires*, XIII. 191.
2. Matthew 18: 35.
3. Luke 23: 34.
4. Matthew 5: 39.
5. Matthew 18: 28-33.
6. Cf. Dean, 101.
7. This criticism of monastic life was strongly attacked during the author's lifetime and placed on the *Index* in Madrid in 1584. (See Battles, 378 n.) Writing to Robert Aldridge in 1527, Erasmus mentioned his *Monachatus non est pietas* as one of the remarks his enemies considered heretical, and ironically supposed that they wanted him to say *Quicunque vult esse salvus, fiat monachus* (Allen, VII, 1858). Years earlier he had insisted that for some people to take up this way of living—and he included himself among that number—was as foolish as bringing an ass into the Olympic race (Allen, II, 447).
8. Horace, *Ars Poetica*, 269.

MIDLAND BOOKS

INDIANA UNIVERSITY PRESS
Bloomington